FINDING FAITH

FINDING FAITH

A NOVEL

C. E. EDMONSON

© 2011 by C. E. Edmonson. All rights reserved.
2nd Printing 2014

Trusted Books is an imprint of Deep River Books. The views expressed or implied in this work are those of the author. To learn more about Deep River Books, go online to www.DeepRiverBooks.com.

No part of this publication may be reproduced, stored in a retrieval system, or transmitted in any way by any means—electronic, mechanical, photocopy, recording, or otherwise—without the prior permission of the copyright holder, except as provided by USA copyright law.

Unless otherwise noted, all Scriptures are taken from the *King James Version* of the Bible.

ISBN 13: 978-1-63269-044-9
Library of Congress Catalog Card Number: 2010909623

*In loving memory of
Ronald Kiyoshi Morikawa,
whose kindness and faith made this world
a better place…*

Finding Faith

One

FAITH COVINGTON HAD never seen her parents cry, not in all her thirteen years on this planet. Instinctively, she turned away. But there was no easy way out. When she looked to her left, then to her right, she saw only the cause of their misery. Shanties made of scrap lumber and cardboard boxes, bits of plastic and canvas tarpaulins extended along the banks of New York's mighty Hudson River for as far as she could see.

The year was 1934 and America was mired in the worst economic depression the country had ever seen. The men and women and children who lived in the shanties—and there were thousands upon thousands of them—had nowhere else to go. Evicted from their apartments and homes, they'd drifted to the river and erected whatever shelters they could. Trying to make a life out of nothing.

Faith felt like she was supposed to cry, too, like crying was expected. But right at that minute, she was feeling lucky. She'd escaped the fate of the dirty-faced children playing alongside the shanties, of the stooped women who bent over small fires, trying to ready whatever meal they'd scrounged from poorly stocked food pantries. Faith and her mother were going to live with an aunt in Pennsylvania. She had never met this aunt, but she'd have a real bed, a roof that kept her out of the rain, and food on the table. Not that her new life would be normal. No, there was no getting back to normal.

It had all happened so fast. Thomas Covington was an accountant, employed for many years at Alexander and Associates, one of the largest accounting firms in New York City. He'd owned the small row house they lived in, sent his daughter to private school, and was the first man on their block to buy a new car. He regularly treated his family to restaurant meals on Sundays after church, going so far as to place his daughter in a class for young ladies so she'd know which fork to use and where to place her knife.

That life was gone. And even if her father found work next week, even if he made a million dollars, there was no going back anyway. Not to Faith's way of thinking. All the certainty—the expectation that one day would follow another and the routine would never change, that she was safe and protected and secure—had vanished. First their bank, Empire National City Bank, had gone out of business, taking the family's life savings with it. Then Thomas Covington had arrived at work one morning to find laborers carting off the desks, chairs, adding machines, typewriters, and file cabinets—everything. Alexander and Associates was officially out of business, fifty years of continual operation and service wiped out in what seemed like the blink of an eye.

Now, standing next to her parents at the ferry dock, Faith wasn't sad, or even frightened. She was mostly numb, and her mind kept returning to a single image, a maple tree in Central Park that she and her mother had come upon during a walk after a bad storm. A lightning bolt had split the tree in half, exposing its inner core, its very heart. Faith felt that way now, as if every secret part of her was exposed. As if there was nothing left to hide.

Or just plain nothing left.

"It won't be for long, my Little Apple. I'll be on my feet before you know it and we'll be together again."

Faith looked up when she realized that her father was talking to her. She reached out to take his hand. That was expected. But she had no words of encouragement and she felt a deep regret, as if their future somehow depended on her making a little speech. She looked out over the flat water of the Hudson River, to a clock tower a mile away and the word LACKAWANNA written in gigantic letters across the face of a stone building wide enough to accommodate six ferry docks.

Lackawanna, Faith knew, was shorthand for the Delaware, Lackawanna, and Western Railroad. She was looking at the railroad's New Jersey terminal, as impressive as Penn Station or Grand Central, or so her mother, Margaret Covington, insisted. Maybe you had to take a ferry to get there, instead of a taxi or the subway, but once inside the station, you could board a train to anywhere in the country, even to faraway California.

But Faith and Margaret weren't going to California, which would at least be an adventure. They were going to someplace called the Pocono Mountains in eastern Pennsylvania, a four-hour trip that would leave them in...

But that was just it. Faith had no clear picture of where she was headed. She had no idea what her life would be like. She was just along for the ride and wasn't expecting any adventures.

Finding nothing to say, Faith put her arms around her father's waist. Thomas Covington looked so much older now. His eyes were swollen with sorrow and fatigue, and his shoulders were slumped. For the past six months, he'd gone out every day except Sunday, searching for a job opportunity that just wasn't there. The unemployment rate, trumpeted in every newspaper, was above thirty percent, which was unheard of. All across the great city, men and women lined up four and five deep, tens of thousands of them, waiting for a single bowl of soup or a slice of bread.

There at the ferry, on her way to her new life, the only time Faith felt like crying was when she looked into her father's face.

As Faith stared across the water, a ferry left one of the station's slips and began its journey across the river toward them. In a few minutes, she and her mother would be on board for the return journey to the New Jersey station.

As she waited, the line for the ferry began to grow and a few children from the homeless encampment wandered over. The children were young, no more than five or six. They approached with their dirty hands outstretched, but they didn't speak and their eyes were as solemn as the eyes of hungry animals. A pair of policemen—big and burly—moved to intercept them, to shoo them away from the good citizens, the ones with the price of a ferry ride in their pockets. A few people threw pennies, which the children scrambled to retrieve.

"Don't be fooled," one of the policemen admonished. "They'd as soon pick your pocket as look at ya."

Faith ignored the comment. She'd begun preparing herself weeks ago—ever since her mother told her they would have to stay with her Aunt Eva on a farm in Pennsylvania—for this moment of parting, when she would step onto the ferry and leave her father behind. She couldn't let anything distract her from that now. Not the kids. Not the cops. Instead, she set her jaw, determined not to cry. Her father was burdened enough—her mother, too—without her adding to their misery.

The effort left her dizzy. Inside, in her heart, the tears were now falling, and her bravado vanished like the country's prosperity. But she somehow managed a smile and her voice shook only slightly when she finally spoke.

"Don't worry about us, Daddy. We'll do okay. Me and Mom, we're tough apples."

The words brought a smile to Thomas Covington's face. Little Apple. That was his favorite nickname for his daughter. It might have been that she was so sweet, or that her cheeks were so rosy, or that her bath powder smelled like apple blossoms, or that she had been brought up in the Big Apple. Or it might just be that Faith was the apple of his eye. But as sweet as Thomas Covington thought she was, Faith had always been fearless, too—climbing every available piece of furniture before she could even walk.

Margaret Covington hadn't much appreciated this aspect of Faith's personality. After all, her daughter wasn't some street urchin, running wild while both of her parents were out working. Thomas Covington was college-educated and Margaret had graduated from high school. They had a position to maintain. Faith would have to become a lady if she hoped to marry well, and a lady she would become.

Margaret was always careful to set the example. Even now, with every available resource already tapped, her green dress, pressed and immaculately clean, fit her slim form perfectly. Her matching, wide-brimmed hat curled down over one eye and looked as if she'd bought it yesterday. Only her tear-streaked makeup betrayed her inner feelings.

They waited as long as they could, letting the other passengers flow around them, until the boatman was about to run a chain across the boarding gate. Then Faith took her mother's hand and they stepped onto the ferry, turning immediately to keep Thomas Covington in sight.

Faith raised her hand to wave as the ferry moved off. They were on the *Ithaca*, one of the fastest of the many ferries that crossed the Hudson. The journey across the river wouldn't take more than a few minutes and Faith wanted to keep her father in sight for as long as possible. She was hoping for a smile, but he seemed to fall apart as the distance between them increased. Tears streamed down his face, and down her mother's face as well.

The realization came slowly, but was no less powerful when it finally hit her. Thomas and Margaret Covington were afraid the separation would drag out—that weeks then months would pass before they saw each other again. Perhaps they even feared a final separation. It happened, Faith knew it did. Unable to find work, to support their families or even themselves, men drifted away to become part of an army of homeless men roaming the country, without ties to anybody or anything.

"I'll see you soon, Daddy," Faith called, the words already out of her mouth before she had even decided to say them.

All around, the ferry's engines throbbed, a steady pounding that overpowered her voice. Her father was already too far away to hear. That was fine. She had meant those words mostly for herself.

Faith watched her father grow smaller and smaller until he finally disappeared from sight. Then she watched the city retreat, the great colossus of Manhattan with its familiar skyscrapers, the Woolworth and Chrysler buildings, the newly erected Empire State Building. It seemed to be growing smaller, too—but it wasn't just the distance.

FINDING FAITH

Thomas Covington had taken his daughter to the observation deck of the Empire State Building shortly after it opened for business. The view from the terrace on the eighty-sixth floor was stunning, and a little scary. The greater world seemed to spread out before her, a dare and a promise at the same time. Faith had dreamed, on that day, that she would somehow conquer the city, would be ushered into its finest restaurants and nightclubs and hotels. She'd dreamed that the life of the city would belong to her—but never dreamed that one day she would be banished from it. That it would have no place left for her.

Faith looked to her right, to the Statue of Liberty in the harbor. The Lady was there, on her pedestal, to welcome immigrants and visitors. Now she seemed to be waving goodbye. To Faith's left, in the distance, the George Washington Bridge crossed the waters of the Hudson like a necklace around the throat of a Fifth Avenue socialite.

Faith was leaving the hustle and bustle of New York's busy streets, the only world she'd ever known. Her destination was a blank slate, an entire unknown, but she was determined to adjust, for her mother's sake, if for no other reason. And so she didn't cry, or even turn for a final look at the city she loved when the ferry bumped to a halt and the passengers began to move toward the shore. She took her mother's hand and walked resolutely forward, through the ferry terminal and into the Lackawanna Railroad Station's vast waiting room.

For just a moment, Faith's mind drifted away from her troubles. The sun was pouring through a stained glass ceiling fifty feet overhead, splashing colored light onto the marble floors, transforming the room's high-backed wooden benches into church pews. But this was no church, a reality she quickly grasped. Two railroad policemen in wrinkled uniforms were moving along the rows, rousing men who were asleep, demanding to see a ticket, sending those who didn't belong on their way.

Faith watched the men shuffle across the floor as her mother retired to repair her makeup. Then they purchased tickets and found seats on a bench. The two policemen approached them a moment later, but didn't ask for their tickets or even hesitate before passing by. Margaret Covington and her daughter were still respectable, at least on the surface.

As though reading her daughter's mind, Margaret cleared her throat and began to speak. Her tone of voice was sure and strong, a tone very familiar to Faith. One of Faith's pet peeves, back when the world was stable enough for minor complaints, was that her mother was always certain of everything. You couldn't argue with her. You could barely discuss anything.

"There's something I want to talk with you about, so that there will be no doubt later on. Even a few years ago, we wouldn't be having this conversation. But you're on the verge of becoming a woman, so I think you should know."

Faith responded with a nod and a simple, "Okay." That her mother's "conversations" tended to be monologues was a fact of life she generally accepted.

Margaret folded her hands in her lap. She was sitting with her knees bent at a right angle, both feet on the floor. Ladies never crossed their legs in public.

"I want you to know that your father and I did everything right. And it wasn't easy, my daughter. Your father went to work when he was seventeen. His parents wanted him to attend college, but they didn't have the money. So, he worked days and studied at night for many years and it nearly wore him out. Your father was in his junior year at

City University when he and I were introduced at a party. I remember thinking that he was the most tired-looking young man I'd ever laid eyes on."

Margaret stopped abruptly, her eyes turning up as she gathered her thoughts. Finally, she continued. "The point is that we were responsible and never asked for any handouts. Your father worked his way through college and then worked even harder after he was hired at Alexander and Associates. And we lived modestly, Faith, putting money aside every month. Many of our friends were heavily invested in the stock market during the boom. They thought we were fools because we put our money in the bank at low interest while they were getting rich. Well, maybe they were right after all," she sighed. "In the end, our money was no safer than theirs. Everybody lost out."

Faith spoke the first thought to enter her head. Until now, the family's finances had been none of her business.

"I don't get it. How is that fair?" she asked.

"That's the whole point, Faith. Fair had nothing to do with our troubles, or anyone else's. A few people made a lot of money when the stock market crashed. They were in a position to see the crash coming. For the rest of us, the Depression rolled over us before we even knew it was there. Our savings would have been enough to carry us for at least two more years if the bank hadn't failed. But the bank did fail and we have to live with the results."

While Faith searched her mind for an appropriate response, Margaret withdrew a long change purse from her pocketbook. She opened the purse and extracted a pair of coins from the very bottom, two nickels. Margaret Covington was a strong woman, but she did have one weakness, which she now indulged.

"You see the newsstand across the way?" she asked her daughter.

"Yes."

"Well, I want you to go over there and pick out two candy bars. We'll need to gather our strength for the trip."

Faith didn't have to be told twice. Nor was she surprised by her mother's parting demand.

"Chocolate, of course."

Two

WHEN A LOUDSPEAKER announced that their train was ready for boarding, Faith Covington followed her mother out of the terminal to the open-air train sheds. She stopped for a moment before they boarded to stare at the massive steam locomotive at the front of the train. The locomotive's driving wheels were taller than she was, and the cab so high that the engineer and the fireman needed a ladder to reach it.

Once again, she sensed the powerful forces behind the changes in her life. There was something out there, certainly larger than she, perhaps larger than all the human beings put together.

Behind her, the train stretched out, its fifteen metal cars with their rounded windows as sleek as a basking snake. Where would they carry her? Into the unknown, into something new, something different. That was all she could say.

"Faith?" her mother called softly.

Faith finally took her eyes off the train and broke away, following her mother into a second-class car, where they quickly found seats. There were signs of neglect there. The chrome trim on the luggage racks was dented, as was the trim around the soiled and scratched windows. The tiles on the floor were old and worn, and the leather seats gave way under Faith's weight. She told herself that the trip would only take four hours. She could put up with anything for four hours.

As she waited for the ride to begin, Faith found herself looking forward, not back. She wondered what Aunt Eva would be like, what the farm would look like. Would there be cows and horses, pigs and lambs? She imagined fields of corn stretching into the distance, plows moving across the land, turning the soil, just like the modern farming methods described by Miss Tredway in her natural sciences class at school.

Faith just started to think about how much she missed that class and all of her schoolmates—well, *most* of them, anyway—when the train's whistle sounded once, then twice, and finally a third time, pulling her back from the past and into the present. A shudder passed through the cars as the great locomotive inched forward. Steam from the engine shot straight up toward the sky then slowly drifted off.

"We're on our way," Margaret said.

Faith looked around her. The train was only half-full, the passengers mostly businessmen in double-breasted suits that had seen better days. Even the conductor's blue uniform, when he collected their tickets, had a tear over the breast pocket. But he was cheery enough.

"Pocono Summit, eh?" he said. "Mighty quiet in Pocono Summit this time of year. Tourist season don't start for another month."

Margaret sniffed once as she took the punched tickets out of his hand. She wasn't going to satisfy his curiosity and so turned her head to the window. The conductor tilted his cap and scratched at his shaggy hair, the expression on his face one of amused indifference.

"Well, little girl," he said to Faith, tipping his hat, "good luck in Pocono Summit."

When the conductor moved on to the next passenger, Margaret turned to her daughter. "In New York, people mind their own business," she said.

"I think he meant to be friendly."

Margaret started to speak, but then stopped. Friendly or not, the effect was the same.

The train was passing through Passaic, New Jersey, an industrial city not all that different from the New York City that Faith knew. Squat, brick factories crowding both sides of a narrow river were flanked by long blocks of attached homes. She could see workmen sitting on crates at the river's edge, enjoying their lunches, and women hanging laundry in backyards. At the end of a broad avenue lined with shops, the steeple of a tall white church stood out against the blue sky.

"Faith, there's something we have to talk about," her mother began suddenly.

"Something else?"

"Where we're going...it's not exactly what you think."

"How do you know what I think?"

Ordinarily, Margaret took no guff from her daughter. Faith had a fresh mouth, as some of her teachers had noted. But now Margaret, as she turned to the window, seemed not to hear the question, so deep was she in thought.

Faith watched her mother with a wary eye. Something was coming, something big. But Margaret didn't turn back toward her daughter. She continued to stare at the houses and factories until Faith relaxed in her seat.

They passed through a number of small towns before reaching the city of Paterson forty minutes later. Paterson was bigger than Passaic, a center for the silk industry on the east coast. It was industrial for the most part, but at one point they crossed a deep gorge with a river at the bottom. In the distance, a waterfall gleamed in the sunlight, its waters dropping eighty feet to the bottom of the gorge. The view was there and gone before Faith was able to take it all in.

"Do you know what river that is?" she asked her mother.
"I'm sorry?"
"The waterfall. You were staring right at it."
Margaret looked at her daughter for a moment. She was a good-looking woman, with a firm brow and brown eyes only a shade lighter than her hair. Ordinarily, she projected firmness and determination, but now she seemed positively grim.

"I was thinking about something else," she said. "Sorry, baby."
"Thinking about what?"
"Something I should have told you about long ago. Something I had tried to put behind me."
Faith was torn between her curiosity and the near certainty that her mother's little secret wasn't one she wanted to know. Over the past year, Faith had developed a sixth sense for bad news.
"I don't think I'm going to like this," Faith said.
"I'm sure you won't, Faith, but the subject can't be avoided any longer. In fact, we're headed right into it." Margaret straightened in her seat and took her daughter's hand. "Let's begin with the simple fact that I'm part...that

you're part…" She paused and cleared her throat. "We're part Indian."

Faith blinked. She wouldn't have been more shocked if her mother had told her that she was part Martian.

"What? How?" she asked.

"My mother. She was part Ojibwa and part Lenape Indian. The Lenape are also called the Delaware, but that's a name given to them by the settlers who drove them out. They never use it themselves." Margaret Covington stopped long enough to shake her head and squeeze Faith's hand. "This is very hard for me."

"After what we've been through, I don't see how anything can be hard," Faith said.

Margaret laughed. "Out of the mouths of babes."

"And that's another thing, Mom. After all we've been through, I'm not a *baby*."

"Okay, fine. You've got to grow up and this is part of the process. My mother passed away when you were an infant and my father went back to his hometown in South Dakota, so you never got to know them. But your grandmother was an Indian and your grandfather was Scotch-Irish."

"How did they get married then?"

"Does that seem impossible? People fall in love, Faith, even people from different races." Margaret paused, but Faith didn't reply. "Anyway, your grandmother chose the modern way. She grew up on a reservation, but she rejected Indian life, for the most part."

"For the most part?"

"Grandma had a sister, Eva, who took the opposite course. Eva chose to live in the Indian way, or as close to it as she could manage. I spent several summers with her…"

"Wait a minute. You're talking about Aunt Eva? The one who's taking us in?"

The train's whistle sounded and the train began to slow as they approached a station. Faith read the sign, TEANECK, as they came to a stop by a stationhouse much smaller than any they'd seen before. As if cued by a movie director, a dozen men emerged from an encampment several hundred yards away. They carried trays on straps hung around their necks and moved from window to window, offering apples and nuts and skinny sandwiches. "Shabby" didn't begin to describe these men. Their clothes were dirty and, for the most part, they were unshaven. One man's shoes were held together with string. Another wore a hat without a brim.

Windows began to shut as soon as the men appeared, but Faith was intrigued. If nobody wanted to buy their goods, why did the men even bother? Her mother didn't close her window, but she didn't offer to buy anything, either.

"They're afraid." Margaret said, without any prompting.

Faith shuddered. There were times when she was sure her mother could read her mind. "Who's afraid?"

Margaret gestured to the other passengers.

"Do they think the men will hurt them?"

"No, they're afraid that what happened to these men will happen to them, too. Keep in mind, not all that long ago, these men probably had jobs and families. Now they've lost everything." Margaret's mouth tightened as she thought of her own husband. Struggling to maintain her composure, she nodded to herself. "Some people think poverty is contagious. They try to keep as far away from it as possible."

A man limped up to the window, an old man; what was left of his hair was now snow white. He was gaunt, with flaring cheekbones and hollow cheeks, and his thin lips were spread in a humorless smile that revealed several missing teeth.

FINDING FAITH

"Buy an apple, ma'am? Help out an old veteran. Only five cents."

Margaret went into her purse, found a coin and laid it on the man's tray. She started to take an apple, but changed her mind. They were too bruised to be eaten.

"Bless you, ma'am." His voice trailed off as he moved to the next window. "Bless you."

A moment later, two railroad policemen ambled out of the stationhouse. Seeing them, the peddlers began to move away. The drama seemed to take place in slow motion, as though all concerned were acting parts in a play they'd performed many times before.

A man sitting in front of Faith turned to the woman sitting next him. "What these bums need," he declared, "is a swift kick in the pants."

"Yes, dear," the woman said, tilting her head in the man's direction. "Whatever you say."

Faith giggled. How to get along with an obnoxious husband was a frequent topic of conversation among her and her friends. Never disagree, that was one way. Men need to be in charge, the reasoning went, or at least *think* they're in charge.

"Mom, why didn't you tell me this before? About you—about us—being Indian?"

"*Part* Indian," Margaret corrected. "But that's not really the point. I was raised as an ordinary American, except for those summers with Aunt Eva on her farm. And when I became old enough to make a choice for myself, I chose the American way of life. Aunt Eva wouldn't put it that way. She says that I chose the white man's way of life. As though I was some kind of traitor."

Faith looked past her mother, out the window. They were passing through farm country now and the carefully tended fields stretched to the horizon. Cows grazed on a hillside. In a fenced paddock, a foal pranced on unsteady legs. Faith watched it trip, fall, get up and trip again. The little horse didn't seem to mind, as its mother didn't seem to notice.

"You'll have to work," Margaret said.

"What?"

"Everybody works on the farm."

"Even the children?"

Margaret smiled. "I thought you said that you weren't a child."

"I'm not." Faith shifted in her seat. "What kind of work?"

"Whatever Aunt Eva tells you to do."

"Aunt Eva's in charge?"

"Oh, yes, my daughter. It's Aunt Eva's farm."

"What about her husband? Does she have children?" Now that Faith had a chance to adjust, her curiosity was running ahead of her tongue.

"Aunt Eva's a widow, and her children have moved away. They've chosen the white man's life, something you don't want to mention to Aunt Eva. But even when Uncle Jonas was alive, Aunt Eva ran the farm. That's another thing about the Indian way. In the old times, women were completely in charge of the farming. Men built the houses, which the women then owned, and they hunted for meat, but women planted and tended the crops. Without them, the people would have starved." Margaret hesitated before adding, "That's what the name *Lenape* means. 'The people.'"

Faith sat back in her seat, her thoughts flying through her head like swirling searchlights at the opening of a Broadway premiere. *Indians? The Indian way of life?* What was it all about?

Thomas Covington loved westerns and he'd taken his daughter to watch dozens of them. Over the years, Faith had seen just about every western actor in Hollywood. Bob Steele and Tom Mix, Randolph Scott, Walter Houston, and Gary Cooper—there was always a new western playing at one or another of Manhattan's many theaters. Not every western featured Indians, but they had only one role to play in the movies that did. Covered with war paint and wearing feather bonnets, they were bloodthirsty savages who attacked settlers, stagecoaches, and cavalry forts, whooping at the tops of their lungs.

Had there ever been a scene in any of those movies showing an Indian farm? Or an Indian doing anything but scalp fallen soldiers? No, movie Indians were all alike. They attacked for no apparent reason and they lost in the end.

"Did Aunt Eva ever go on the warpath?" Faith finally got the courage to ask.

Margaret laughed for the first time in weeks, a laugh that came from deep inside. "Aunt Eva's always on the warpath," she announced when she caught her breath. Then she turned serious. "I know this is hard for you, honey. I know that. And I would never have subjected you to Aunt Eva's way of life if... The truth is that we have no other choice. Your other aunts and uncles have problems of their own. They couldn't take us in."

"But not Aunt Eva?"

"That's the funny thing, Faith. Aunt Eva didn't hesitate when I wrote to her. She said that sharing was the Indian way, especially when it came to family. I was her sister's only child and there would always be room for me and my daughter in her home."

An hour later, Faith asked to go to the observation platform at the end of the car just to stretch her legs—but really she wanted to clear her mind. She was surprised when her mother agreed, and even more surprised when she was allowed to go by herself. Maybe this was part of becoming a woman. If so, Faith wasn't about to complain.

She walked down the aisle, threw open the door at the back of the car, and stepped onto an open-air deck. The view from there was broader than the view through the car's dirty windows. Nevertheless, it was anything but encouraging. They were passing through a region of low mountains, snaking around and between the peaks. To either side, a forest—dark and thick—pressed to within fifty feet of the tracks. When they crested one of the lesser mountains, the view was of a virtually unbroken wilderness that ran all the way to the horizon. She could count the tiny farms dotting the landscape on one hand.

Faith was dismayed. She was in real-life wilderness!

Oh, sure, that was just great. Did she look like a pioneer? Was she supposed to be Lewis or Clark?

Faith could distinguish between a dessert fork, a shrimp fork, and a dinner fork. She'd been taught never to begin eating until everybody was served and her hostess began to eat. She knew how to fold a linen napkin, to take small bites of her food, and to return the napkin to the table unsoiled. But what good would that do her here? The forest was a world entirely unknown to her and they were heading deeper and deeper into it with every mile. There didn't seem to be any end to it, as there seemed to be no end to the Covington family's troubles.

As Faith considered her situation, the door to the facing car, a first-class car, suddenly opened. A young girl, perhaps ten years old, accompanied by a middle-aged woman, stepped onto the facing platform. The girl wore a wool crepe dress, pearl gray, that fit her so perfectly that Faith knew it was hand-tailored. Her hat, of the same color and material, had just as obviously been created by a milliner. Faith's bonnet, on the other hand, had been purchased at Macy's. And none too recently, at that.

"Hi," the girl said, giving her perfect blond curls a little shake. "My name is Pauline."

The woman standing behind the girl emitted a little grunt of disapproval, but Faith paid no attention. In a cheap cotton dress and the plainest of sturdy brown shoes, the woman had to be the governess. It was her job to be displeased.

"Hi," Faith returned. "I'm Faith."

"Don't you just hate train rides, Faith? Soooooo boring. I much prefer touring by car," the girl said precociously.

Faith didn't know exactly how to respond. Her family's trips, once to Cape Cod, once to Niagara Falls, twice to Atlantic City, were wonderfully exotic treats. Faith had looked forward to each and every one. She would have walked if that were the only way to get there—to say nothing of riding in a first-class train cabin.

"Where are you going?" Faith finally asked.

"Pocono Summit." Pauline rolled a pair of sad blue eyes before repeating her favorite phrase. "Soooooo borrrrrring."

"I'm going there, too," Faith said, though she realized they were headed to the same place under much different circumstances. "My mother and I are going to stay with my Aunt Eva."

"I'm staying with my father for the summer. His name is Jaspin Gore. He's in mining."

What could Faith say to that? My aunt's in the business of scalping settlers? Instead, she asked, "Are you traveling with your mother?"

Pauline's eyes softened and, for a moment, Faith was certain she would cry. But she only said, "My parents are divorced." Then she smiled. "My father has a summer home on Wildwood Lake, but I hope we don't stay there all summer. It's soooooo borrrrrring. I hope we move to Scranton. That's where my father really lives. In a house with so many rooms I still haven't seen them all."

Faith stopped listening, though the girl went on and on. A breeze had sprung up while they were talking and the topmost branches of the surrounding forest were gently swaying. Beneath her feet, the hiss and clack of the train's wheels continued on, relentlessly, indifferently. Equally indifferent, the clouds above cast vast, moving shadows on the treetops. In the far distance, the waters of a lake reflected a white-hot drop of light.

"I've got to go," Faith said, a bit abruptly. "My mother's probably getting nervous by now."

"Maybe we'll see each other in Pocono Summit," Pauline said brightly.

Faith noted the look of grim disapproval on the face of the girl's governess. The woman's nostrils were so pinched that Faith didn't see how she could breathe. No, a friendship between the daughter of a man whose home had too many rooms to count and a beggar who couldn't afford to put a roof over her head was quite out of the question.

Three

THE TRAIN CONTINUED on through the mountains for another hour, stopping at stations so small they seemed like mere afterthoughts. Faith Covington couldn't imagine anyone disembarking there—not without a compass, a sleeping bag, and maybe a machete, anyway.

The forest remained unbroken, stolid, and dense—as immovable as the face of a rocky cliff. Faith sat beside her mother, her hands folded in her lap. She had a million questions, but was too afraid of the answers to ask them.

At the front of the car, two soldiers were drinking from a pewter flask. Suddenly, they began to sing, slurring their words, much to the disgust of the other passengers. Over and over, they sang the opening verses of "Happy Days Are Here Again," all the while conducting a vigorous argument about the lyrics. Finally, the conductor entered the car and asked them to keep it down. The minute he was gone they started up again, this time choosing "On the Sunny Side of the Street."

Faith was less than thrilled at the impromptu performance. Both songs suggested that folks ignore the grim realities that marked day-to-day life in New York City—the mass evictions, the homeless children living in packs, the bodies lying frozen in the streets on cold winter mornings. Just grab your coat, get your hat, leave your worries on the doorstep. Nothing to it.

Maybe, on her best day, Faith could manage to forget her troubles, but this was not her best day. No, this was about the worst day of her life.

These thoughts were still running through Faith's mind when the train finally cleared the mountains and began a long descent into the valley. For a time, the tracks ran alongside a broad river marked by rapids wherever it narrowed to sweep around mid-water islands. A dozen canoeists had taken advantage of the spring floods. Maneuvering their canoes through the roughest spots, they braved the turbulent white water. Faith watched, fascinated, as one of the canoes flipped, its nose rising straight up before it landed on its side, throwing its two paddlers into the roiling water.

At first the paddlers were helpless, despite their life jackets. Faith knew how they must have felt.

The water was moving too fast for swimming. It spun the men around, tossing them from side to side as if they were twigs. Then the river suddenly widened, the waters calmed, and the men swam into a quiet backwater. Their canoe, unfortunately, had other ideas. It was headed downriver. Fast.

"What river is that, Mom?" Faith asked.

"The Delaware. It runs all the way to the Atlantic Ocean."

"And that house over there?" Overlooking the river, the house Faith pointed at was midway up a steep bluff.

Enormous by any standards, it featured a row of eight, white-brick chimneys that ran the length of the building's slate roof. "Who lives in that house?"

"That's Cliff House. It's a resort."

"People stay there?"

"Of course. People from the coast have been coming to Monroe County for their summer vacations for a long time. Why not? The scenery is beautiful and the summers are much cooler than in New York or New Jersey."

"Aren't we in New Jersey?"

"Not for long. That's Pennsylvania on the other side of the river."

Faith stared out the window as the train turned onto a stone bridge. From the center of the bridge, she could see a dozen resorts on the Jersey and Pennsylvania sides. Faith was cheered by the sight. She'd nearly given up hope, but here it was, civilization. She could live with this, even if she was asked to wash dishes and make beds. Even if she was asked to clean bathrooms. Though she'd much prefer to curl up in front of the radio or lose herself in a book, hard work didn't frighten her. What frightened Faith was that unbroken wilderness, that forest as dark as it was unending.

In East Stroudsburg, a few minutes from the bridge, the train stopped long enough to take on water for the engines. Margaret and her daughter took advantage of the delay to quench their thirst with a treat: two bottles of Coca-Cola purchased at a small grocery store. As they strolled back to the train, Faith again fought an urge to ask specific questions about their final destination. Unfortunately, her mother was doing her mind-reader act again. As she and Faith slid their green glass bottles into a wooden crate, Margaret spoke without looking at her daughter.

"Where we're going," she announced, "is nothing like this."

Despite Margaret's warning, as the train cruised first through a valley then began a long, slow haul to the crest of a mountain, Faith focused on the resorts to either side of the tracks. Spragueville, Henryville, Cresco, Mount Pocono… Faith counted more than two dozen large hotels and many more country boarding houses. The resorts were surrounded by spacious lawns and gardens, swimming pools, even a small golf course. Nevertheless, she had to admit, the train stations themselves were growing smaller with each stop, and Pocono Summit, when they finally pulled in at two o'clock, was the smallest of all. Unpainted for many a season, the stationhouse was little more than a shed.

Next to the stationhouse, on a small, gravel-covered lot, two vehicles sat thirty feet apart. The first was a brand new Cadillac limousine. Every inch of the limousine's black paint gleamed with polish, as did every spoke on its wire wheels. The chauffeur in his gray-green uniform was equally spiffy. The peak on his cap positively glowed.

Not fifteen feet away, an older man wearing canvas pants, dusty boots, and a white undershirt that had seen better days leaned against the rusted fender of an ancient Chevrolet pickup truck. The man's skin was a deep mahogany and his mostly gray hair, braided on both sides, hung below his shoulders.

Faith didn't have to ask which vehicle was waiting for her and her mother. She watched Pauline emerge from the first-class car, accompanied by her governess, and run over to the Cadillac limousine. Naturally.

Pauline was fast, but not as fast as the chauffeur, who opened the car's rear door just before his little mistress plunged inside. An instant later, before her governess joined her, the window on the far side of the Cadillac rolled down and Pauline's face appeared.

"Oh, Faith..." Pauline waved gaily. "Do you see this car? Soooooo borrrrrring. I've been after my father to buy a Packard but he won't hear of it. Well, goodbye. The train was late and my governess insists that I nap before I dress for dinner."

The limousine's engine was so quiet that Faith didn't realize it was running, not until the vehicle described a wide circle, its tires crunching over the gravel, and pulled onto the road. Faith watched the car turn left and quickly accelerate. A moment later, it was gone.

"Faith," Margaret said, drawing her daughter's attention, "this is Ben Hightower."

Ordinarily, Faith would have responded with a little smile and a pleasant hello. But the man with the braids, Ben Hightower, stretched forth a well-callused hand for her to shake. Women didn't shake hands with men, at least according to Miss Jennifer Thompson. "It's never done, girls"—that was how she dismissed any behavior deemed unladylike. It's never done.

Faith looked to her mother for a signal, but Margaret was staring into the distance, apparently unaware. Finally, Faith took Ben's hand—she could hardly leave it dangling in space—and squeezed gently.

"Pleased to meet you," she said.

"Yes, pleased to meet you."

Though Ben's expression didn't change, Faith recognized a hint of amusement in his tone. Most likely, he wasn't used to polite conversation.

She watched him gather their bags, noting that despite his age, he was agile and graceful, his back straight, his stride firm. He tossed the bags into the truck's bed as if they weighed no more than feather pillows, and then got into the driver's side.

Again, Faith was taken by surprise. In polite company, men always opened the door for women. Now she watched her mother open the passenger-side door and signal her to get in.

Faith did as she was told, squeezing in next to Ben Hightower, while her mother took the window seat.

"All ready?" Ben asked. He pressed the starter button and twisted the key without waiting for an answer and the truck roared to life. And "roared" was exactly the right word. If the pickup truck had a muffler, it wasn't functioning. The noise was ear-splitting and Faith flinched involuntarily.

"Been meaning to fix that," Ben said. When he rammed the shift stick into first gear, the crunch was louder than the steady chug of the engine.

Faith felt her heart sink. What was she doing here, in her neat dress and her sun bonnet? How could this have happened? She'd been trained all her life to be a lady and she could curtsey with the best of them. So what? Her entire childhood was now irrelevant, all her skills rendered useless by her family's unexpected, and undeserved, poverty.

Up until now, she'd more or less assumed that she was in control. Sure, she messed up from time to time, but the messes were of her own making. She had the power to correct them, or at least try not to get caught next time. Now she felt like a leaf in the wind or those canoeists she'd seen on her way here—whipped here and there by the wind or the water, a prisoner of circumstances so powerful that she could barely comprehend them.

Four

BEN HIGHTOWER MANEUVERED the pickup through the lot and onto the road, following the path of Pauline's Cadillac limousine, long ago lost to sight. A marker by the side of the road read: "SR 115." Faith Covington assumed that SR meant "state road" and she wondered why the road had a number and not a name. But she didn't raise the question with her mother or Ben Hightower. There was no point. That was their road and they were going to take it: name, number, or nothing.

They drove the first several miles through a resort area. Most of the inns were little more than Victorian houses with deep gables and porches that wrapped around the fronts of the buildings. The one exception was the Pocono Manor Inn. With its fieldstone walls and rounded corners, the manor resembled a medieval castle. Faith spied a small lake behind the house.

For just a moment, she was cheered, but then the resorts dropped away and the forest pressed in on both sides of the narrow road. To her, the woods seemed impenetrable. The branches of the smaller trees intertwined at the level of her head and every inch of ground was covered with brush.

Thankfully, her mother's attempt at conversation took her mind off the forest for a moment.

"Well, Ben, how have you been?" Margaret asked.

"I'm doin' okay."

"And Aunt Eva?"

"Eva's her usual surly self." Ben's small mouth broadened slightly. He might have been smiling. He might have been nursing a toothache. Faith couldn't tell either way.

"That bad?" Margaret asked.

"Eva is what she is. I'm not expectin' her to change. No, ma'am."

Margaret turned to her daughter. "Ben's been staying with Aunt Eva for years. They're a team."

Staying with Aunt Eva? Talk about never done! In Faith's world, a respectable woman would never think of sharing a house with a man she hadn't married.

"What do you do?" Faith asked Ben.

"Whatever Eva tells me to."

Ben and Margaret laughed, sharing a joke lost on Faith. Back in New York, there was a word for husbands who were bossed around by their wives: "henpecked." Only Ben wasn't Aunt Eva's husband. He was some kind of employee, maybe like a ranch hand in a western movie. But in the movies, ranch hands were always white and Ben Hightower was definitely a red man. He had the small eyes and broad cheekbones of movie Indians, and his expression, now that he'd settled down, was so composed that New Yorkers would probably assume he'd lost consciousness.

"I guess I don't have to ask how you been," he said to Margaret. "From what I'm hearin', things are mighty rough in the cities." Ben shifted into third gear and the truck—though it blew out a cloud of black smoke in protest—slowly accelerated.

"'Mighty rough' doesn't begin to describe the situation," Margaret said, her voice flat. "New York is falling apart. We're just part of the rubble."

Ben ignored the bitter tone. "I remember them summers you passed with us, Margaret...remember 'em real well. Yes, ma'am. You were a might spunky, if I do say so. Spoke up, too, and ain't too many folks speak up to Eva. Way I see it, you'll do fine. You got grit."

"Thanks for that, Ben. I only wish I was as certain."

Faith looked past Ben and out the window as they passed a small house. The house, and the little clearing it stood on, was gone in an instant, and they were back to the forest. This time, though, Faith managed to pick out a few details. First thing, the leaves on the trees were tiny, unlike the forest in the valley, where the leaves were fully developed. They were high up on the mountain now, and the effects were plain to see.

"Is spring always this late?" she asked.

"The winter was cold," Ben explained. "Still had ice on the lake two weeks ago. But it's warmed up now."

"Did Aunt Eva get her crop in yet?" Margaret asked.

"Just gettin' started."

Faith spotted a line of small trees in full blossom, their branches lined with clusters of small white flowers. "What are they called?" she asked.

"Juneberry," her mother replied.

"Make good eatin' when the berries are ripe," Ben added.

"And those?" Faith gestured to a patch of yellow blossoms growing in the open space beside the road. The flowers were butter-bright in the sun.

"Wintercress," Margaret responded.

"Scurvy grass," Ben quickly added.

Faith shuddered. Scurvy? Wasn't that a disease that British sailors got?

"Does wintercress make you sick?" she asked.

"Just the opposite," Margaret said. "Late winter was always a hard time for Indians, especially up here where the first frosts come early. Without green vegetables, the people suffered from a number of vitamin deficiencies, especially Vitamin C, which causes scurvy."

Faith was impressed—and more than a little surprised—that her mother knew so much about plants. Back home, she couldn't even keep a house fern alive.

"And wintercress contains Vitamin C?" Faith asked.

"Exactly. The plant begins to grow very early in the spring. In the old days, the people were more or less desperate for green vegetables by then." Margaret looked at Ben. "But that was the Indian way of life. Feast or famine."

"What does…scurvy grass taste like?" Faith asked.

Ben spoke without turning his eyes from the road. "That, Miss Faith, you'll find out for yourself. We'll be eatin' it tonight."

They drove on for another fifteen minutes, occasionally passing a few small houses, until they finally came to a Texaco gas station. By then, steam was leaking out from beneath the Chevrolet truck's hood and the needle on the gas gauge was pointing to empty. Ben pulled inside, settling the truck next to a bright red gas pump. The pump was crowned with a circular crest displaying the familiar Texaco star against a white background. A sign just beneath the crest announced the price: "12 CENTS/Complaints Extra."

"Twelve cents a gallon," Ben complained as he opened the door. "It's ten cents in Stroudsburg."

An attendant came out of a repair bay, wiping his hands on a greasy rag, only to have Ben wave him away.

Ben took off the Chevrolet's gas cap himself and inserted the pump's nozzle into the neck of the gas tank. He started the gas flowing just as a V8 Oldsmobile sedan pulled into the station. The passenger-side door opened almost before the car stopped and a man got out, leaving his companion behind the wheel.

The man was tall and lean, with muscular arms that he folded over his chest. He wore a gray cap pulled down across his forehead, which was low to begin with, and his left cheek bore a long, jagged scar. Faith watched from inside the pickup as he ran a finger along the scar. Though the man didn't speak, not at first, his bad intentions were obvious. The look on his face was scornful in the extreme.

Ben pumped five gallons of gas into the pickup, and then went inside for a water can. He returned and opened the hood, never so much as glancing at the Oldsmobile sedan or the man who leaned against it.

"Hey, Hiawatha, you been on the warpath lately?" The man brought his fingers to his mouth and let out a whoop. "You scalp any peaceable settlers?"

Very carefully, Ben took a rag out of his back pocket and removed the radiator cap, unleashing a plume of white steam. He stepped away from the car and shoved the rag into his pocket.

"Not talkin'? Oh, yeah, now I remember right. You're one of them silent injuns. Lemme hear you say, 'Ugh.'" Overcome by his own wit, the man began to laugh.

Faith listened in disbelief. The tension she felt was completely unfamiliar. Was this what it meant to be an Indian? Why didn't Ben respond? Even her mother was responding; she had rolled down the window and stuck her head out with her sternest stare, which had always worked on Faith—no words necessary.

Faith could feel the outrage. Ben had done nothing to provoke this attack. But even now, as he poured water into the radiator, his features were composed. If the man's taunts were reaching him, he gave no indication.

"I got it, injun. Lemme hear you say, 'How.'" Pleased with himself, the man repeated the word, dragging it out: "Howwwww!" That brought another laugh. "Say, I hear there's work for ya down in Cresco. Ol' Karl Stamford's decided to go into the cigar business. You could be his cigar store injun. Oh, but wait, you injuns don't like work, ain't that right? You all just wanna run through the woods, shootin' squirrels and such. Mighty warriors."

Faith felt like she couldn't breathe. She watched Ben as he replaced the radiator cap and carried the water can back into the station. He reached into his pocket, came out with a handful of coins, and handed them to an older man who was busily repairing a tire. Ben was on the way back when the man leaning against the Oldsmobile spoke again.

"Guess you're doin' right well these days." The man paused long enough to glance at his companion in the car before delivering the punch line. "But I do gotta say that you're gettin' too long in the tooth, old man, to be totin' around *two* squaws. Seems like one'd be enough."

Faith felt her heart drop. Somehow, without her knowing it, she'd become an Indian. And this, apparently, was how Indians were routinely treated.

Faith's mother had spoken about choosing to live in the American way, about how Aunt Eva considered her a traitor. That was ridiculous. The surprise was that anybody would choose to live as an Indian.

Still, Ben didn't react, not until the man took a step toward him. Then he reached calmly into the pickup's bed and withdrew an axe handle. The handle was split on the end that would have held the axe head, but it was perfectly suited to the task at hand. Ben held the wooden handle with both hands at a diagonal across his chest. He didn't speak, but his expression hardened. That he'd made a decision to fight was as obvious to Faith as it was to the man with the scar, who stopped in his tracks.

"What you gonna do with that?" he asked.

"Put your hands on me, Crease Marron, and you'll find out."

The man inside the car broke the tension. Faith couldn't see him, but his voice carried across the open lot.

"Get back in the car, Crease. Now."

That was all the excuse that Crease Marron needed. He spit on the ground, a lot closer to his own feet than to Ben Hightower's, before rejoining his companion. A moment later, the Oldsmobile sedan disappeared around a curve in the road.

"I'm sorry, honey," Margaret whispered to Faith as Ben got into the truck. "I'm sorry for dragging you into this. I had no idea."

Faith almost spoke the words on the tip of her tongue, but she checked herself at the last minute. She wanted to ask, *What choice did you have?* But she knew the question would only make her mother feel worse.

Ben started to put the Chevrolet in gear, but Margaret twisted the key in the ignition, shutting the truck down.

"Don't think you can just drive off without an explanation, Ben Hightower," she said. "Because I won't have it. This was no random encounter."

Faith marveled. Her mother rarely disagreed with her husband, and when she did, it was only in the most careful and measured tones. Though Faith was still trembling, she realized, dimly, that there were aspects of her changed circumstances that she might be able to live with.

Faith, like most of her girlfriends, didn't relish the prospect of spending the rest of her life trying to please a man, but there just didn't seem to be any way out of it. At least in the world she'd left behind.

"I'm thinkin' you'd best hear the news from Eva," Ben said. He started the truck and shifted into first gear, but didn't take his foot off the clutch. "That man who come out of the Olds, Crease Marron, he's deputy constable for the township. The other one, his name is Abe Hoskins. He's the constable. Crease is a mean son-of-a-gun, but his boss is the dangerous one."

Faith spoke up first. New York City was divided into five boroughs. *Township* was a totally unfamiliar concept.

"What's a township?" she asked.

"Pennsylvania is divided into counties," Margaret said, "and the counties are subdivided into townships. We're in Albemarle Township, which is part of Monroe County."

"And a constable is like a policeman?"

"There's a county sheriff, but he spends most of his time in Stroudsburg. That's the biggest town, where most of the tourists go in the summer. Constables only have authority in the townships," her mother explained.

"How many constables are there in...Al-be-marle Township?"

"One constable," Ben said as he revved the engine of the Chevrolet pickup truck, "and one deputy constable."

Now it was Margaret's turn. "So, all right, Ben, out with it. Why did that deputy constable challenge you? Why did he talk to you that way?"

Ben shifted gears, taking his time, and the engine roared as the little truck accelerated, giving him another excuse for delay. Finally, he said, "It's the same old story, Margaret. If an Indian has somethin' white people want, they take it."

"What do they want this time?" Faith asked.

"Land, same as usual. The land we been livin' on for a hundred years. My parents and grandparents are buried on the shores of Wildwood Lake. Me, I always planned to join 'em there."

"And this is what they're doing, harassing you?"

Ben finally shook his head. This was as far as he was prepared to go. "If you don't mind, I'll leave Eva to tell you the rest. Eva likes to talk."

Satisfied, Margaret leaned back and put her arm around Faith's shoulders. They were passing through a stretch of unbroken forest, mile after mile of trees and brush. The sun was directly overhead and its beams passed through the leaves of the hardwoods to dapple the forest floor with light. The alternate pattern of light and shadow fascinated Faith, and she was a bit cheered simply to discover that light actually reached the ground. From the train, it had seemed as if the sunlight were being absorbed by the upper branches of the trees and everything below would be in darkness.

They drove on for another fifteen minutes without passing a house. The only evidence of human activity were the NO HUNTING signs nailed to the trees closest to the road. And even those were few and far between. Faith was beginning to wonder if the forest stretched clear to California when a lake came into view.

"Hold up for a minute, Ben," Margaret said. She waited until Ben pulled onto the margin of the road and set the handbrake. "That's Wildwood Lake, Faith. That's where we're going. Wildwood is the largest lake on the Pocono plateau, and the deepest, too."

Despite her mother's enthusiasm, Faith wasn't all that impressed. Her family had visited Lake George in the Adirondack Mountains a few years ago and Lake George was much bigger. In fact, New York's harbor alone was big enough to swallow a dozen Wildwood Lakes. Plus, there wasn't a home in view; the lake appeared to be surrounded by unbroken forest. Nor were there any boats on the water, or any sign that humans had ever been there, only birds, dozens and dozens of them, scattered across the placid, sun-swept surface. Faith recognized Canadian geese and some of the ducks—she'd seen them often enough on the tiny lake in Central Park—but the other kinds of birds were completely unknown. She watched them for a minute as they dove underwater then resurfaced, only to dive again a moment later.

"Look there, Faith." Margaret pointed to a paved road that disappeared into the trees surrounding the lake.

"Is that the way in?" Faith asked. "Why can't I see any houses?"

"You can't see any houses because they're hidden by the trees. The property owners wanted to preserve the wild view. As for your first question, that road is, indeed, a way into the community. Just not into our community, which is at the other end of the lake. You see, Wildwood Lake has become a hunting and fishing preserve for a few of Pennsylvania's most powerful families. I don't like putting it that way, but there's no way to get around the facts. We were here first, but we live by their rules. Except for a few thousand acres to the east, which is our little world, they control all the land for miles around."

Faith shifted in her seat. "Do you mean people like Jaspin Gore?"

"Miss Faith, how do you know about Jaspin Gore?" Ben asked.

"The girl at the station, Pauline. She told me that she was Jaspin Gore's daughter."

Faith looked out over the lake at a flock of geese descending one by one, their honking calls as penetrating as they were raucous. The geese were hitting hard, sending up sprays of water. Faith watched the flock swim in circles for a moment, until all had landed. Then they came together, forming a wedge, before swimming toward the far end of the lake.

"What would happen," she asked, "if we took that road?"

"There's a guard post a few hundred yards in. It's still there, right?"

"Still there," Ben said.

"Well, if we took that road, we'd be turned back unless we lived, or worked, there," Faith's mother continued. "We have to use the road at the other side of the lake. The two roads don't connect. We have our road and they have theirs."

Ben put the truck in gear and they drove for another few minutes until they came to a second road, this one unpaved and marked by deep ruts and exposed rock. Smiling, Ben spun the wheel.

"Almost home," he said as they slowed to a crawl.

Five

THE SHORT TRIP, less than a mile, took nearly twenty minutes to complete. The well-worn springs on the old pickup truck weren't adequate to the task of negotiating the ruts and the rocks. That was obvious enough. But the road wasn't adequate, either, and when they encountered another vehicle, a dilapidated Model A Ford, Ben was forced to pull onto an open space beneath an enormous beech tree.

The Model A was driven by a tall man whose brush-cut hair grazed the roof. He waved to Ben as he passed and Ben waved back. This little dance was apparently very common. Still, Faith Covington raised a question.

"What do you do when it's raining and the road's muddy?" she asked.

"Depends," Ben replied.

"On what?"

"Well, if you're talkin' about a passin' storm, folks just stay home 'til the road dries out. Winters, though, are different, what with all the snow we get. And spring, too, when the snow melts. No, winter time, we mostly leave the cars out by the main road and walk in."

But Faith wasn't through. Between New York City's subways and its many buses, the city was up and running every day of the year. That was part of New York's get-ahead attitude. You never let anything hold you back. Certainly not a narrow road. In New York, there was no such thing.

"What if there's an emergency? What if someone has a heart attack and you have to call an ambulance? How does the ambulance get to the patient?"

"That can't happen, honey," Margaret said, her voice gentle, "because there's no telephone service. The state hasn't run the lines yet."

No telephone? What year are they living in here? Faith wondered. She looked at the poles by the side of the road, at the wires strung between them. *Well, at least there must be electricity. We won't have to sit in the dark. Probably.*

They passed a number of small houses, perhaps a dozen in all, as they made their way to the farm. The modest homes were only a couple of hundred yards apart and a number of them appeared to be abandoned. They stood in clearings, often with a garden and a few outbuildings alongside. A few had smoke rising from chimneys. In others, women toiled in the gardens. The women stood to wave as the Chevrolet pickup passed, and to scrutinize Margaret and Faith. In a small community like this, Faith realized, everyone knew everyone else. Her arrival—and her mother's—came as no surprise.

So, what exactly was expected of Faith Covington? Because there would definitely be expectations, she knew that. It was like switching schools or moving into a new neighborhood. You had to figure out where you fit in with everyone else around you. Not that it was easy… Far from it.

FINDING FAITH

Faith's thoughts were interrupted when Ben stopped the car and pointed to a dead tree by the side of the road. The tree was still standing, though there wasn't a speck of green on any of its limbs and its bark was sooty black. Perched on one of the tree's highest branches, a large owl, perhaps two feet high, stared over the top of the pickup. The owl's gray head was almost perfectly round and its oddly flattened face appeared to melt back on itself. A series of feathered circles, divided by a hooked beak, lent the bird's face a sleepy appearance, except for the close-set yellow eyes. Those eyes were entirely awake. Awake and watching.

"The owl has secrets," Ben said. "If she whispers her secrets in your ear, you can see the future."

"Please, Ben," Margaret broke in, "don't fill her head with that nonsense." She turned to her daughter. "The Lenape have a story for every occasion. They use stories in place of science."

"I thought owls were nocturnal," Faith said, drawing on her own knowledge from science class.

"Some are, but not all," Ben said. "Some are very active during the day. And some come out when they want to tell you something."

Margaret shook her head, but nothing more was said.

A few minutes later, they reached their destination: Eva Darkcloud Benton's home at the end of the road. To Faith, it really was the end of the road. The end of life as she'd known it, at least.

Aunt Eva's single-story house was bigger than most. A small chicken coop stood in one clearing. A larger building stood midway between a shed and a barn. And Aunt Eva had a garden, surrounded by a head-high fence made of chicken wire, that covered most of an acre.

A tall, stocky woman rose to her feet as they approached. She had a hammer in one hand and clasped a dozen nails in the other. Behind her, the fence had buckled and a section was almost touching the ground.

"Bear came through last night," Ben explained. "Knocked the fence down. Don't know why. There's nothin' in there to eat, not 'til the crops come in. Reckon that bear was just feelin' ornery. Don't like nobody messin' with his forest."

Margaret opened the car door. "You listen to Ben," she said to Faith as they got out, "and you'll think every animal in the forest is a genius. You'll think the animals have more politics than Washington, D.C."

Faith paid no attention to her mother. The woman marching toward them—her Aunt Eva, no doubt—was wearing overalls. Women usually didn't wear pants. But here came Aunt Eva, gray ponytail swaying, work boots slapping, the top two buttons of her work shirt undone. No makeup, of course, and no hat, no jewelry, no purse. Aunt Eva was a big woman, taller than Faith's mother, maybe taller even than her father, with wide shoulders and broad hips and a round belly the approximate size and shape of a small watermelon. Though her face and neck were wrinkled and she appeared to be at least in her sixties, there was nothing feeble about her long stride.

"Margaret, welcome," she said. "And you, too, Faith."

"Thank you for having us," Faith said, standing alongside her mother. "I'm pleased to be here."

"Somehow, I doubt that. But here you are anyway." Aunt Eva looked Faith over. "Tell me, do you do well in school? Are you smart?"

Faith gave the questions a moment's thought. In fact, she did very well in school and she did consider herself to be smart. She just couldn't say it out loud.

"Bragging isn't polite," she said.

"Not polite? Indians brag about everything. And why not? Nobody's gonna brag for you. But I can tell right away that you're smart and that you know it, too. So listen carefully to what I'm gonna tell you. You're up here in the middle of nowhere on this rundown Indian farm and you maybe feel like your whole life has fallen apart. But what you need to do is make the best of the situation. You don't learn from doing the same things over and over again. All you do is get yourself in a rut. But now you have an opportunity to learn, a real opportunity. So, listen close and don't be too quick to judge."

Margaret rolled her eyes. "Same old Aunt Eva," she said. "You might have saved the speech for dinner."

"Same old Margaret," Aunt Eva returned. She met Margaret's eyes momentarily then returned to Faith. "The few summers she spent here, your momma couldn't wait to get away. Personally, I don't blame her. Life up here is about hard work and little reward. And I don't expect you to become an Indian, either. I met your papa once and I know him to be a good man. He'll find his way before long. He'll find his way and you'll be leavin' soon enough. I'm hopin' you'll take what you learn here with you."

Faith tried to frame some sort of response, something besides, "Yes, ma'am." But she had no idea what she was supposed to learn and she was still too shocked by Aunt Eva's general appearance to concentrate on her advice. One thing, though, did strike her. Woman or not, Aunt Eva was in charge.

"I'll try," she finally said.

"Good, good. Now you take the rest of the afternoon to settle in. You can work tomorrow. Today, you can explore a bit, but you don't want to be wanderin' into the forest. If you're not friends with the forest, you can get lost real easy. Every year some fool tourist dies in those woods."

Though Aunt Eva's last warning rattled her a bit, Faith shook it off. In fact, she felt relieved to discover that the house included running water, a real bathroom, and a kitchen sink. But there was no living room, only a large kitchen with a table and chairs, a refrigerator, and a huge, wood-burning stove.

"Lands, I did grow to hate this stove," Margaret said. "At first, everything came out either burnt or raw. I couldn't maintain a constant temperature in the oven."

"But you learned," Ben said.

Margaret wasn't consoled.

"You remember how that thing works?" Aunt Eva asked with a grin.

"I think so. Is the firewood still in the same place?"

"Yep."

Margaret and Ben led Faith to a small bedroom on the opposite side of the house. There were two narrow beds with iron headboards in the room, a dresser that looked as if it might disintegrate if somebody sneezed too hard, and a single lamp on a small table. Home sweet home.

"You ladies gonna be okay?" Ben asked as he set the luggage down. "'Cause I get to get up on the roof, fix a leak around the chimney. If I don't get it done 'fore dark, there'll be grief to pay."

"We're fine, Ben," Margaret said. "You've been a dear, as always. Anyway, I've got to get the stove going if I'm to help make dinner."

Faith followed her mother into the kitchen—it seemed all she did was follow—and opened one of the kitchen cabinets. The dishes inside were plain white and many were cracked at the edges, but they were clean and neatly stacked.

"Is this your job?" she asked her mother. "Are you the housekeeper?"

Margaret laughed. "Don't look so unhappy. We're not guests here. We're family. That's why we're expected to work. In Indian families, except for the very young and the very old, everyone contributes. Personally, I'd rather take over the cooking and cleaning than work in the garden. I don't especially care for dirt and digging. Now, you go outside and explore a bit. Aunt Eva was right when she said there was plenty to learn."

Faith passed the remainder of the afternoon in a daze, her attention wandering from one unfamiliar object to another. Her mind was still jammed with questions, but she didn't want to bother Aunt Eva or Ben. Aunt Eva was in the garden, turning the earth with a spade. Ben was up on the roof, spreading tar at the junction of the roof and the metal chimney pipe. Margaret gathered wood from a pile heaped against the side of the house.

Faith watched as her mother sliced off small bits of kindling with a hatchet and slid the kindling into a paper bag. Watching her mother cut down the entire tree herself with a pair of sewing scissors wouldn't have been much weirder. The bag, along with a few larger chunks of wood, went into a wicker basket that Margaret carried to the house.

For a time, Faith settled herself on the stump of a tree felled long ago. She tried counting the growth rings, as Miss Tredway had taught her, but lost count after twenty. She considered fetching a book from her suitcase in the bedroom. Reading is what she usually did when she was alone with time to fill—reading or listening to the radio. But there was no radio here and no comfortable chair to curl up in.

Faith leaned forward, dropped her elbows to her knees, and cupped her chin with her hands. Before her, a dozen chickens prowled the hard-packed yard, scratching at the ground, always on the move. To Faith, their activity seemed random at first, but then she happened to be looking when a red hen snatched an insect from a clump of grass. The hen swallowed the insect in an instant, and then went back to work trying to find another one.

In fact, Faith realized, all the hens were working. What had seemed random to her at first was intensely purposeful. What's more, the birds remained vigilant throughout, raising and twisting their heads, always on the lookout for danger. Their feathers were a deep red-orange, their small tails a blue so dark that in the shadows they appeared black. A rooster, his much larger tail held proudly aloft, watched over the hens, only occasionally showing any interest in the ground.

As Faith continued to watch, Ben climbed down the ladder. He crossed the yard to a hand pump over a well and washed his hands.

"Aren't you afraid the chickens will wander away?" Faith asked him.

"You mean wander into the forest?"

"Yes, that they'll want to become wild again."

"Miss Faith, every living thing in these parts that eats chickens lives in that forest. And them chickens, they know it."

"How could they know if they've never been in the forest?"

Ben sighed. "Now, see, right there? If I answer that question, I'll be crossing your momma. She never did care for loose talk about Indian spirits. So, I'm just gonna say that we never had a chicken go wild. They know what they gotta do to survive. Come sundown, when it's feedin' time, they'll go back in the coop on their own."

FINDING FAITH

Ben retreated to the small barn, carrying the bucket of tar with him. Faith rose from her seat a moment later. With nothing special in mind, except to see what was there, she circled the house. She found a path in the back, well-trodden, that curled between long-needled pine trees in the shadow of a small grove. She took a dozen steps on the path then stopped to look over her shoulder, only to discover that she could no longer see the house. Her first thought was to make like a chicken and dash back the way she'd come, but then, suddenly, her troubles closed in around her.

So much was gone, vanished, as Aunt Eva's little house had vanished. All her friends, including her best friend, Emma Thornton, were lost to her, almost as if they'd never existed in the first place. Schuyler Academy was the only school she had ever known, a refuge from the teeming public schools. She would never return there, she knew that—even if her father managed to find a job. Her home, too, would be repossessed in a few days, repossessed and sold to someone else. Faith had explored every inch of its three stories, had made a nest—a reading nook—for herself in the attic, had overcome her fear of the dark in its windowless basement.

All her life, Faith had felt safe and protected. One day ran into another and the months and years built upon themselves, forming a clear, clean path from baby to adult. She'd never dreamed, not in her worst nightmare, that her safety could suddenly be taken from her. And now what? Would she spend the rest of her life digging around in the dirt? Aunt Eva's so-called farm was no more than a grubby homestead hacked out of a dark, impenetrable forest. What was it Ben said? Everything that eats chickens lives out in those woods? And Aunt Eva, too. Every year, she'd claimed, some tourist got lost in the forest and didn't come back.

Faith thought about retracing her steps. But there was nothing behind her that she wanted to see. Maybe she'd be better off wandering into the woods, just another foolhardy tourist. Hesitantly at first, then faster, she continued along the well-worn path, thinking she was headed into the forest. But then, just a few seconds later, she found herself on the edge of the expanse of Wildwood Lake.

Faith scanned the shoreline, but couldn't find a single house. The only sign of human life was a canoe pulled up between some rocks. The life of the lake, on the other hand, was obvious at a glance. Six little turtles had arranged themselves in a line on what remained of a tree that had fallen into the water. A small island, thirty feet from where she stood, supported a mound of dried mud from which dozens of tree branches protruded. Faith recognized the mound for what it was, another legacy from Miss Tredway's natural sciences class. She was looking at a beaver lodge.

Most of all, there were the waterfowl, including the familiar geese, and mallards, too, with their iridescent, blue-green necks and chestnut wings. Faith had seen mallards on the lake in Central Park many times. But there were other species swimming on this lake. The first to catch her attention was a cluster of small birds with starkly divided black and white heads. Then she turned to a group of four birds with long, orange crests. Each of them swam alongside smaller birds with dark blue heads and white bodies. Mated pairs, Faith assumed, going about their business.

But that's what all the birds were doing. Though some appeared to be resting while others dove beneath the water in search of food, every single one of them was going about the business of survival. Were they at the end of a long migration from some warm southern state? Or did they have further to go, maybe all the way to Canada, perhaps even above the Arctic Circle? And what had they endured?

How many times had they flown through heavy storms, or fought high winds, or been shot at by hunters, or attacked by hawks? They couldn't complain, of course, or even imagine that things might be different.

They could only accept the hardships that came their way and carry on.

Six

FAITH COVINGTON REMAINED by the side of Wildwood Lake for almost an hour, until she heard her mother calling her name. Margaret Covington's tone was tinged with enough anxiety to motivate Faith as she hustled back along the well-worn path. When she burst into the yard, she found her mother standing near the chicken coop. Her face was red and she stood with her head cocked to one side and her hands on her hips.

"Where were you?" Margaret demanded.

"By the lake."

"Why didn't you tell me you were going?"

"But you told me to look around."

Faith found the give and take, so very familiar, to be comforting. At least one thing hadn't changed. Her mother fretted whenever she was out sight, or so it seemed. Maybe that didn't speak well for her becoming an independent adult, but right now independence was the last thing she wanted.

"Well, dinner's ready." Margaret finally let her hands fall to her side, though she didn't smile. "Such as it is."

Aunt Eva blessed their food before they ate. She gave thanks for what little they had, and then expressed her faith that the Lord would provide for them in the future. Faith listened attentively, thinking, *So far, so good.* But then Aunt Eva asked something named *Mess-en-goo*—at least that's what it sounded like—to make sure the animals in the forest had enough to eat. That was so they'd be nice and fat when it came time to hunt them.

"Amen."

Faith looked at her mother, but Margaret simply shrugged. She'd already warned her daughter about the Indians' belief in spirits. The odd part was that Aunt Eva and Ben had long ago converted to Christianity. According to Margaret, they'd twisted their new religion to accommodate the old beliefs, had changed Christianity's very nature. Faith was told to pay Aunt Eva no mind.

Too hungry to pursue the issue, Faith turned to her dinner. Big mistake. Dinner was some kind of green leaves stewed with white beans and a bit of meat, and a platter of corn bread. The meat was tough and dry, despite the hours in the pot, and the greens were so bitter that Faith shuddered when she bit into them. She looked to her mother, who raised the question on the tip of Faith's tongue.

"What are we eating, Aunt Eva?" Margaret said.

"Wintercress and dandelion greens, spiced with wild onion and wild mustard. And, of course, Mexican white beans from last year's crop."

Faith had been chewing a bit of meat for several minutes, grinding the morsel between her back teeth in a fruitless attempt to break it down. Finally she just swallowed.

"What kind of meat is this?" she asked.

"Venison, dried in the fall." Aunt Eva smiled. "Try the corn bread. Your momma made that."

The adults went back to eating and a moment later they were discussing the Whitehorse family, who'd sold their land to a company named Scranton Properties before moving to Oklahoma. Nobody paid any attention to Faith, not even her mother. That was unusual in itself because her mother usually encouraged her to eat.

Though it took some thinking, Faith eventually got the point. She didn't have a lot of options here. Dinner was on the table. She could eat or go hungry; it was strictly up to her. Well, at least the corn bread was good.

The conversation grew more animated after her mother served dessert, some kind of squash pudding flavored with hickory nuts. This was more to Faith's liking, though it didn't compare with the pastries her father picked up on their way home from church on Sundays. As she ate, she began to listen more closely to Aunt Eva's tale.

Scranton Properties, it seemed, had made offers to every Indian family on Wildwood Lake, generous offers that exceeded the value of the individual properties, especially in these hard times. The company's motive was obvious to Ben. Most of the land surrounding the lake was owned by wealthy white families. They now wanted the rest. This was an old, old story, hardly worth repeating.

Aunt Eva was more suspicious. Indian families, she pointed out, owned thousands of acres, but only a small fraction of that was lakefront property. So, why the rush to get them out?

"As you can see from the meal," Aunt Eva said to Faith, finally including her in the conversation, "we're pretty self-sufficient. Almost everything we eat, we grow, hunt, or gather. But there are still things we have to buy, and taxes we have to pay in the fall. Most of the families raise money by working in the resorts during the summer. I have a stand in Mount Pocono near the train station where I sell Indian souvenirs. I wouldn't exactly call it a living, but it pays the bills. Or at least it did in the past."

Aunt Eva paused for a moment then turned to Margaret. "The tourist industry is way down. Half of the smaller inns have already closed and there are more to follow. If the folks behind Scranton Properties just waited until tax time, they could most likely pick up some of the land for a song. Me, I'm askin' why they're in such a rush. And why the harassment? Why would Constable Hoskins, who never bothered with us before, help Scranton Properties to get us out? No, there's somethin' else happening and I mean to find out what it is."

Aunt Eva looked at Ben. "And there's another thing I'd like to know," she went on. "The white families only come up here in the fall to hunt and fish. You cross into their part of the lake, you'll find every home empty except for one. That would be Jaspin Gore's. Now, why would Gore be up here all by his lonesome in the springtime? It don't make sense, none of it. But I'll tell you one thing sure. I'm not plannin' to leave any time soon. If Scranton Properties wants my land, it's gonna have to come up with something a lot more persuasive than money."

Faith found herself listening closely as the discussion continued. Again, Aunt Eva appeared to be in charge. And her determination to remain where she was came as especially good news. If Aunt Eva sold her house and land and moved away, Faith and her mother would have no place to live. They'd be homeless.

Aunt Eva's farm was the one thing separating them from a shantytown. And, for that, Faith felt her first bit of affection for the place.

At least until night came.

FINDING FAITH

Faith had always been proud of her ability to sleep through anything. Police sirens, fire engines, the clang and bang of buses and trucks, the crash of the subway cars running along the elevated line on nearby Third Avenue, even the loud conversations of late-night drinkers returning from the clubs and bars—she could handle anything the city threw at her. Now the sounds of the country found her wide awake. First, there was a shrill peeping that rose and fell from moment to moment, then an occasional ghostly trill that came from a great distance and spoke of sorrows too awful to contemplate. But the most disturbing call—*hoo, hoo, hooooooo*—sounded right outside the room's only window. Listening despite herself, Faith was unable to shake the feeling that the calls were somehow addressed to her.

Across the room, Margaret Covington was sound asleep. Faith supposed her mother had simply gotten used to the din when she'd lived with Aunt Eva. Or maybe she was just worn out. The day had been long and difficult.

Lying on her back, eyes open, Faith wondered how her father was doing. All of the family's many problems rested on his shoulders; the solutions could only come from him. The burden must be crushing. And what could he do but apply for the same jobs at the same companies that had already rejected him?

Faith imagined her father trudging along the sidewalks of New York City, unwilling to spend the nickel it cost to ride the subway or take a bus. He would never give up, not while there was life in his body. Everything her father had acquired, everything he was now in danger of losing, he'd gotten the hard way. He was a battler. But, of course, that didn't mean that he'd win the battle. Faith remembered all those tents and shanties by the Hudson River, remembered the men and the women and the children living in those tents. Surely, there were battlers among them, too. Only, they had been beaten.

Suddenly, and without analyzing the consequences, Faith slid from beneath the blankets and rose to her feet. The temperature outside hovered near fifty degrees and it was no warmer in the little bedroom. The woodstove in the kitchen was the only source of heat, and it had long grown cold. Beneath Faith's feet, the floor was freezing and her arms were instantly pimpled with goose bumps. She was tempted to jump back into bed, but she resisted. Instead, she slid into her shoes, wrapped a blanket around her shoulders, calmly walked to the window, and lifted the shade.

The moon was up, a half-moon suspended in a black sky imprinted with millions upon millions of stars. The silver band of the Milky Way formed a distinct path directly overhead, the highway of the ancient gods. On the far side of Aunt Eva's garden, the forest's edge marked off the boundary of the known world.

Hoo, hoo, hooooooo. The call sounded again, two quick syllables, followed by a final, drawn-out entreaty.

Faith's eyes moved to the source of the call and found, on a branch overlooking the garden, an owl bathed in moonlight. Maybe not the same bird she'd seen earlier, but definitely the same species. That round head and that oddly divided face with its concentric half-circles? There could be no mistake. It looked as if the animal's head had been taken apart then sewn back together along a seam. But there was one thing she hadn't noticed before. The bird's gray feathers weren't tight against its body, but hung down loosely, like a cape or a cloak, reaching almost its feet.

The bird was looking directly at Faith, who assumed that she'd drawn its attention when she raised the shade. Wild animals were supremely aware of their surroundings. If not, according to Miss Tredway, they generally got eaten.

But the owl didn't seem especially threatened. Just the opposite. The bird was watching and waiting, as unmoving as a stuffed owl she had seen on a field trip to the Museum of Natural History.

What the bird was actually waiting for became obvious a moment later when its wings unfolded and it rose from the branch, gliding silently over the wire fence surrounding the garden, dropping suddenly to the earth then rising again, a small animal hanging from its sharp talons. Life for one creature was death for another.

Faith watched the owl rise, its wings flapping slowly, deliberately, until it cleared the tops of the trees. Then the owl was gone, back to its nest, perhaps to feed its young. It was spring, after all.

Faith let the shade down and returned to her bed. Within seconds, she was sound asleep.

Seven

FAITH COVINGTON AWAKENED to the crowing of the farm's rooster. Though it was barely dawn, when she glanced at her mother's bed, she found it empty and made. The window shade was up, too, another hint. Aunt Eva's farm wasn't given to leisure; there was no radio, not even a phonograph player. Work was the name of the game.

Nevertheless, Faith fell back on the pillow and closed her eyes, remembering the night sounds and the owl with its odd, cloak-like feathers. In the picture books she'd read as a young child, the owl was always portrayed as a fountain of wisdom, the creature other animals sought out when they had a problem they couldn't solve on their own. But the owl Faith saw seemed to had been about solving one problem and one problem only—how to capture a meal. Still, those close-set yellow eyes had seemed to look right at her.

"Faith, rise and shine."

Faith opened her eyes to find her mother at the foot of the bed. A pair of overalls was draped over Margaret's arm. A pair of boots dangled from her right hand. The boots and overalls were both new and obviously meant for Faith Covington.

"Am I supposed to wear those?" she asked.

"Yes, I'm afraid." Margaret tried to smile, but couldn't quite pull it off. "You're to work with Aunt Eva in the garden. She wants help with the planting. I can't say as I blame her. Aunt Eva's closing in on seventy years old. If she had any sense, she would have given up the farm long ago."

"Lucky for us she doesn't have any, then."

"Oh? Well, if I were you, I'd watch my smart mouth around Aunt Eva." Margaret paused, but her daughter remained silent. "Breakfast is almost ready. I've got to get back to the stove before the eggs burn."

Left alone, Faith pulled on the unfamiliar, boyish clothing and headed for the bathroom where she washed her face and brushed her teeth with water so cold it made her jaw ache. She found herself thinking she'd have to be a polar bear to get into the bathtub, but she didn't worry for long. It was too cold to even attempt it. She hurried toward the warmth of the kitchen, and then stopped in her tracks as the mingled odors of brewing coffee and pan-fried eggs flooded her nostrils. No boiled greens? No rock-hard bits of dried venison? She could live with that.

In fact, it turned out that venison was included in the meal. Thin strips fried up until they were as crisp as bacon. There was hot corn bread as well, slathered with some kind of red jam. Faith took a bite and smiled.

"What's on the bread?" she asked.

"Choke-cherry preserves," Aunt Eva replied. "I put 'em up last summer."

"Choke-cherries? Do they grow wild?"

"Sure do. Free for the gatherin'."

Faith dug into her eggs. They were delicious, as was everything she put into her mouth, including the bacon, and she didn't stop until a cup of coffee was put in front of her. This was something entirely new. Tea and coffee were drinks for adults. Faith looked at her mother for guidance, but Margaret was cracking eggs into a frying pan and didn't turn around.

"Aunt Eva," she said, sipping cautiously, "I couldn't sleep last night."

"And why's that, honey?"

"There was so much noise."

Across the table, Ben laughed gently. "Back when I was in the army, I was stationed in Philadelphia for a month before I was shipped overseas to fight in the war. Swear to the Good Lord above, I couldn't sleep more than ten minutes for all the commotion in the city. Now here you are, complainin' about noise in the country."

Faith helped herself to another slice of corn bread, covering the yellow surface with choke-cherry jam, but she didn't eat. "I guess," she told Ben, "it depends on what sounds you're used to. There was this screeching that never stopped, like millions of insects. I felt surrounded."

"Those weren't insects," Ben explained. "You were hearin' frogs."

"Frogs?"

"Tree frogs. We call 'em spring peepers. Mostly, they ain't much bigger than a thumbnail. Make a heck of racket, though."

Faith nodded to herself. *Frogs that climb trees? What's next? Flying turtles?* "There was another sound. I can't describe it very well it because it was so weird. Sometimes it sounded a little bit like yodeling. But, most often, it was like somebody calling from the other side of the grave."

"Did the sound come from the lake side of the house?" Ben asked.

"I think so."

"Then I suspect you were hearin' a loon."

"A loony?"

"No, a loon, a water bird." Ben stopped for a moment, and then made a sound exactly like the call Faith heard the night before. "That sound right?"

Out of words, Faith nodded once before returning to her breakfast. Time to let go. But Aunt Eva couldn't resist a little jab.

"No loons in New York?" she asked.

"No, Aunt Eva...and frogs have the good sense to stay out of trees."

To Faith's surprise, and relief, Ben and Aunt Eva roared with laughter.

Breakfast done, Faith left the house. Aunt Eva was still discussing the day's work schedule and her mother was busy with the dishes, so she went alone. She hadn't taken two steps into the yard when she was stopped in her tracks. There so many birds singing so many different songs, their music seemed to come from everywhere at once. Faith searched the grounds and the trees at the edge of the forest, somehow expecting to find thousands of animals perched in their branches. But except for a robin hopping across the hard-packed earth and the foraging chickens, there wasn't a bird in sight. Not only that, but the birds stopped singing when she came through the door, at least the ones closest to the house, only to start up again a moment later. Faith had been scrutinized. Scrutinized and judged to be no threat. Now it was back to business, the business of singing, though why birds should waste their time singing was a mystery. Just like the rest of her new life.

Satisfied, Faith walked to the edge of the woods where she carefully examined the smooth gray bark of a tree that leaned into the open yard. No spring peepers. She turned to a second tree. There, the rough bark hung from the trunk in shaggy strips that appeared ready to pop off. In fact, the ground at the base of the tree was littered with bark. But still, there wasn't a frog in sight.

Faith was about to conclude that she'd been bamboozled when a small flowering plant growing between two black rocks caught her eye. The blossoms were as small as they were simple—five white petals with pale yellow centers, perhaps an inch across. With the sun still rising behind the trees, the flowers were in deep shadow, yet Faith was immediately drawn to their quiet perfection. At the base of their stems, the dog-toothed leaves were the color of the finest green jade in the Metropolitan Museum's collection. Faith dropped to one knee and gently ran her fingers over the leaves and the flowers, so caught up in the moment that she was completely unprepared for her Aunt Eva's voice.

"Strawberries."

Faith flinched. Somehow, Aunt Eva had snuck up behind her. "Strawberries?" she asked.

"Yes, wild strawberries."

"Can you eat them?" Faith wanted to know.

"The sweetest strawberries on the planet grow wild, honey. They're just very small and there are usually not enough in one place to pick. But we got to get to work now. I want to put as much seed into the ground as possible this morning. I got other things to do in the afternoon."

Faith trailed Aunt Eva to the side of the small barn, thinking that at least Aunt Eva might have asked her if she was ready to work, or even if she wanted to work at all. But, no, Aunt Eva had spun on her heel and stalked off.

"Take this spade." Aunt Eva handed Faith a long-handled shovel with a pointed blade. "Now, you see that heap over there?"

Faith looked toward a mound of dirt about thirty feet away. "That?" she asked.

"That's our compost heap. I want you to fill the wheelbarrow about halfway and carry the compost into the garden."

With that said, Aunt Eva snatched up a second spade and a heavy pickaxe then headed for the garden. Faith watched her go for a moment before laying her own spade in the wheelbarrow and taking hold of its handles. Though she'd never touched a wheelbarrow in her life, she wasn't expecting a problem. You pick up on the handles and roll it on the front wheel. Easy. But the wheelbarrow refused to trace a straight line, wobbling to one side or the other every time it met the smallest obstacle. Faith got it done, though, finally dropping the wheelbarrow within a few feet of the compost.

When Faith jammed the spade into the pile, it easily penetrated the loose black compost. No problems so far. She brought the spade to the bed of the wheelbarrow and turned it on its side, spilling out the dirt. And that was it, the whole task. Nothing to it. Nothing at all, until the fourth spadeful produced two of the longest, fattest worms Faith had ever seen. She dropped the spade and jumped back.

"Aunt Eva," she called, "there are worms in your dirt."

Faith's accusation was met with a moment of silence. Then Aunt Eva said, "What were you expecting?"

"Well, certainly not frogs," Faith returned. "They live in trees."

This time, Aunt Eva didn't laugh. "I've no time to play with you, girl. You just bring those worms, along with anything else you find."

Though she shuddered at the prospect—she'd always hated creatures that slithered beneath the ground—Faith picked up the spade and went back to work. When the wheelbarrow was half-full, she jammed the spade into the piled compost and grabbed the handles.

Unfortunately, Faith was totally unprepared for the weight and the wheelbarrow didn't move the first time she lifted. She bent forward, putting her back into the task, and yanked with all her strength. The wheelbarrow rose a few inches then toppled onto its side, spilling the compost onto the ground.

"You might wanna try makin' two trips," Aunt Eva called from inside the garden.

Faith swiped at her hair, which had fallen into her face. She was already perspiring and the day was just getting started. This time more careful to center the load, she followed instructions and was able to push the wheelbarrow into the garden. A few minutes later, after a second trip, she watched Aunt Eva use the pickaxe to break up the ground then separate out the small rocks.

"I tell you, Faith," she said, "seems like there's more stones than soil sometimes. Now, throw in a shovelful of that compost and I'll show you how Indians plant."

Faith did as she was told and watched Aunt Eva mix the compost with the turned earth then build a small mound. She poked a hole in the top, added a few kernels of dried corn and finally covered the hole.

"You know how corn grows?" she asked.

"On stalks?"

"That's right, and the stalks grow straight toward the sun. That's the secret. When the corn gets a few inches high, we'll plant beans—white beans and pinto beans. Beans grow on a vine that wraps around the stalk, which keeps 'em off the ground so they don't rot. Last thing, once the beans have started, we plant squash. The squash puts out thick leaves that keep down the weeds and shade the ground, holding in the moisture."

Aunt Eva rose to her feet and winked. "You want to hear the best part?"

"Sure."

"The best part is that once all the plantin' is done, the garden takes care of itself. Unless we go a long time without rain, I won't pay the garden any mind 'til it's ready to harvest." Aunt Eva grinned, pleased with herself. "Maybe Indians work hard, but they're not about makin' extra work for themselves. Now, what I want you to do is build the mounds and plant the seed while I turn the earth and add the compost."

"You mean with my hands?"

"You afraid of getting your hands dirty, Faith?"

"No, it's not that."

"Then what's botherin' you?"

Faith was beside herself. "Aunt Eva, there are worms in there."

"And thank the Lord for that. Worms don't live in ground that ain't fertile."

"But suppose I touch one?"

"Worms don't bite." Aunt Eva hesitated, but Faith neither spoke nor bent to her assigned task. Finally, her expression grave, Aunt Eva nodded to herself before speaking. "Indians don't care much for tellin' other people what to do. We mostly figure folks can think for themselves. So, I'm not gonna tell you to work. But you need to understand somethin'. The way of life we've been forced into, there's no extra floatin' around. If you don't contribute, the whole family's gonna be on short rations."

Faith shuddered, knowing she would have to work. Maybe Aunt Eva wasn't giving orders, but the way she put the situation, refusal was impossible, not least because it would shame her mother. With a sigh, Faith shut her eyes and thrust her hands into the earth. Big mistake. In her mind's eye, she imagined worms by the dozen crawling over her fingers. She opened her eyes finally, and reluctantly went to work, molding the mixed earth and compost into a mound roughly the size and shape of the one that Aunt Eva had made.

The sun, rising like a ball of red gold, had risen from behind the trees to fix her in its heat, and sweat was streaming from her hair onto her face. She had to resist the temptation to wipe the moisture off with her dirty hands.

"Guess this is pretty hard for you," Aunt Eva said. "Not like your life in the big city."

Faith shook her head, but continued to work, careful to check for worms before sculpting the mounds. They were moving right along, though, despite her reluctance.

"I don't see why you do it," she finally said. "Why you live this life."

"Not every Indian does, Faith. Fact, most Indians live like everyone else. And when they do go into farming, they farm the modern way, with plows and tractors."

"But not you?"

"No, honey, not me."

Faith poked a hole in the top of the mound, dropped in a few seeds and finally covered the hole, careful not to tamp down the earth too hard. If the dirt above the seed was too hard, the seedlings couldn't break through.

"Can I ask why? Being an Indian seems to make everything in life harder," Faith said.

"I been expectin' you to ask this question and I'm glad you did it sooner rather than later. Shows you got grit. But the answer? Well, there ain't no one answer." Aunt Eva dug a shallow hole in the earth, broke up the clods with the edge of her spade and added a spadeful of compost. "For one thing, I like to get close to the ground I'm plantin' in. I want to be next to the ground, to feel the dirt, to smell the earth, not up in some tractor smellin' gasoline exhaust. And then you got to worry about the price of your crop when it comes time to sell. Prices go up and down and you don't have any control. What I'm doin' now is growin' what me and Ben can eat. You and your momma, too, now that you're here."

Aunt Eva watched Faith mix the compost into the turned earth then form a mound. The finished product was a little too small, but she didn't correct her grandniece. "Some people just have a longin'," she said. "An itch they got to scratch. The Lenape were evicted from their lands over and over again, along with the other eastern tribes. Evicted and scattered to places like Wisconsin and Oklahoma and Texas and Missouri and Ohio. There was even a settlement in Canada. It's still there, far as I know, but that's not the point. During their wanderings, the People mingled with many other tribes, and with whites, too. Right now, there's hardly an Indian alive who can claim to be pure Lenape. And our ways got mixed up, our spirits with other spirits, and our ceremonies with other ceremonies."

Faith listened closely, but chose not to speak. Her life, at least before the Depression smashed into it, revolved around her family and her close friends. A very small world compared to Aunt Eva's. Aunt Eva spoke of the People as if she and the tribe were the same thing.

"That itch I talked about?" Aunt Eva said. "I was born in Oklahoma, in what was then called Indian Territory. There were so many tribes out there it was like a League of Nations. Me, even as a young girl, I wanted to come back to my homeland. And I ain't kiddin' myself, neither. I'm doin' the best I can to live in the Lenape way, but what I'm doin' ain't all that close to the way of the Ancestors."

"But you did come home, right?"

Aunt Eva laughed. "Afraid not, honey, not on this mountain. Lenape men traveled up this way to hunt from time to time, but they lived in settlements down by that river you come across on the train. Problem is, the land down there is too expensive. This was the best I could do."

They took a break, then, crossing the yard to the outdoor well. Aunt Eva worked the pump handle until water finally gushed out. Then she filled a tin dipper and passed it to Faith.

"Taste this."

The water was pure, delicious, and so cold it instantly cooled the girl down. Faith handed the dipper back to Aunt Eva and said, "What you said before, about spirits…"

"Yes?"

"Well, at dinner last night, you asked the Lord to bless the meal." Faith paused. She was trained to be polite and that meant not asking difficult questions. Besides, the spring breeze was blowing over her face and through her hair, a breeze as cooling and delicious as the water from the well. "I guess that means you're a Christian, right? But Christians don't believe in Indian spirits, do they?"

"Oh, no? And I suppose Jesus didn't cast out devils? If devils ain't spirits, what are they? And that goes for angels, too. Bad spirits and good spirits, that's what it comes down to. Plus, there are ghosts. Lenape believe the spirits of people and animals don't always pass over. Sometimes they continue right here on earth."

"I don't believe in ghosts," Faith replied.

"Well, there's plenty of good Christians who do. But that ain't the heart of it. Just like the Lenape religion got mixed in with the religion of other tribes, it got mixed in with Christianity. In fact, those who turn their backs on the Indian way, first thing they do is purify their religion. They get right orthodox."

Aunt Eva stopped there. She took a large blue handkerchief from the back pocket of her coveralls and folded it once, from corner to corner. Then she rolled it into a bandana and tied it around Faith's head. "That'll keep the sweat out of your eyes," she told the girl. "Now, what say we get back to work? That soil won't turn itself."

Faith touched the bandana as they crossed the yard. She couldn't shake the feeling that Aunt Eva wanted to make her into some kind of an Indian. Well, that wasn't going to happen. No, sir, no way. Having an Indian grandmother that you never even knew didn't make you an Indian, not by a long shot. Still, she was intrigued by her aunt's comment about demons and angels. If they weren't spirits, what were they?

"Do you go to church, Aunt Eva?"

"Most every Sunday. Immanuel Lutheran Church in Mount Pocono. Pastor Moore is a good man. Knows his Scripture, too."

"What does he think about spirits?"

"Prob'ly nothin', since I never bring the subject up. Pastor Moore's right sensitive and I don't wanna hurt his feelin's."

Aunt Eva's laugh boomed out, startling a pair of crows perched in the upper branches of a sugar maple. The crows were large and jet-black, yet Faith had been completely unaware of their presence until they called out in protest as they flew off.

"Look, Faith, there's somethin' I been meanin' to mention and them birds reminded me. A boy's comin' here this afternoon, a boy name of Paul Crow. Paul's about a year younger than you, but he knows these parts as well as anyone up here. I asked him to show you around."

Faith stopped in her tracks. A boy? Twelve years old? Faith didn't know a single twelve-year-old boy who wasn't a complete pest. Especially when they thought they knew more than she did.

"You might not care for company so soon," Aunt Eva continued, "but I'm hopin' you'll treat Paul kindly as a favor to me. There's not many children his age 'round here and I expect he's right lonely."

"Why are there not many children?"

"Because our sons and daughters leave the mountain soon as they're grown and the ones left are getting too old to have children. I lost two children myself. They went to work for Mr. Henry Ford in Michigan when they were eighteen. They write me letters now."

Faith opened her mouth to speak, only to find herself struck dumb. The look on Eva Darkcloud Benton's face was so full of regret, so sorrowful, that for once in her young life, Faith Covington was speechless.

Eight

SEVERAL INCHES SHORTER than Faith Covington, Paul Crow was a wiry, muscular boy with inky-black hair that hung to his shoulders. He was wearing a tan leather vest trimmed in blue feathers. The expression on his face was so studiously neutral that he appeared grave, and his dark brown eyes were penetrating. He seemed neither unfriendly nor especially eager to make friends. He was just there, waiting for whatever came. But this odd indifference wasn't the worst of it, not for Faith. Paul Crow was carrying a rifle, holding it against his chest with the barrel pointing toward the sky.

Lunch was barely over and they were standing near the garden. Paul had emerged from the forest, his approach soundless. Though he'd raised a hand as he approached, he hadn't smiled.

"You're not going to shoot me, are you?" Faith asked.

"Uh-uh. I'm hopin' to catch me a fat porcupine in the open. Make for a good dinner."

"You're going to shoot a porcupine?"

"If *Mesingwe* allows it."

"Who?"

"*Mesingwe*." For just a moment, Paul looked puzzled, but then he recovered. Faith was from the city. She didn't know. "*Mesingwe* watches over the wild animals. He protects them."

"But not from you." Faith raised her eyebrows and tried to suppress a smile.

"*Mesingwe* knows that humans have to eat…animals, too. But he demands respect, for himself and the animals both. If you don't respect him, he can do you harm."

Aunt Eva stood a few feet away, listening closely. Paul Crow was one of those rare children who came into the world already grown up. To Aunt Eva's mind, he was way too serious. But that was his nature and she would never try to change him.

"Well, I got work to do," Aunt Eva said. "Paul, why don't you show Faith around? And remember, she's a guest of the community. You know what that means, right?"

"Yes, ma'am," Paul returned.

A moment later, Paul and Faith were alone. Faith was still wary. Except for cops and criminals, people in New York didn't carry guns.

"So, what do you want to do?" Faith was still wearing her coveralls and she felt self-conscious, though Paul seemed not to notice. Perhaps he was used to seeing women in pants.

"There's a place I think you might wanna see. It's about an hour's walk."

His proposal laid out, Paul settled back to await Faith's response. She could agree or refuse or propose something else. The decision was entirely up to her. For her part, Faith was intrigued.

"How far is an hour's walk?" she asked.

FINDING FAITH

"Couple of miles. Not far. We'll go fishin' after we get back, maybe catch us some dinner."

"All right, let's go." Faith spoke without really making a decision. She was expecting her companion to lead her to the road, expecting a leisurely walk through the community. Paul Crow had other ideas. He walked directly across the yard and plunged into the woods. Faith hesitated for a moment. She wanted to follow, but her feet seemed to be weighted down. The forest was so, so dark. Not only that, it went on almost forever. That little fact was made clear on the train ride from New York.

Paul's face appeared from behind the trunk of a tree. "It's okay," he said, "if you don't want to go."

If Paul's voice had contained even the slightest trace of contempt, if he was dismissing her, Faith would have turned and walked back to the house. But Paul's tone was neutral. He seemed prepared to respect whatever decision she made. Faith recalled her earlier conversation, when Aunt Eva said that Indians don't tell each other what to do. Maybe that was some kind of rule.

Faith shook her head. "No," she said, "I'm coming."

Five minutes later, Faith was totally lost. She had no idea where she was, no idea where Aunt Eva's house was, or the road, or any other sign of civilization. Paul Crow was moving right along, guiding her through a maze of brush and branches and fallen trees. Unlike Faith, he didn't stumble over roots or trip over rocks. He was at home.

Faith persisted without complaint for the next fifteen minutes, until she was out of breath. Then she called for a break and asked a question that'd been on the tip of her tongue for quite some time.

"Do you know where you're going?"

Paul seemed puzzled again. "Sure." He was still holding the gun against his chest.

"How, Paul? How do you know? It all looks the same to me."

Paul laid the gun against the trunk of a tree then squatted down. "Well, it isn't all the same." He pointed to a tree about thirty feet away. "That's a beech tree. Beech nuts are good, but they're hard to get out of the shell." His finger moved ten yards to the left. "And that's a white oak. You can eat the acorns, but you have to wash out the bitterness. And that's—"

"Wait." Faith held up her hand. "Are you telling me you know every tree in the forest?" Faith waited until Paul shook his head. "If you don't know every tree, how can you tell where you're going? That's the question I'm really asking. Because, truly, Paul, I do not want to get lost and spend a night in these woods."

"I'm following a trail."

Faith's head swiveled from side to side. When she spoke, she tried to keep her tone free of sarcasm, but didn't entirely succeed.

"What trail? Is it invisible?"

Paul rose to his feet and motioned for Faith to follow. He led her to a briar fifty feet away and pointed to a tuft of brown and white fur caught in the plant's thorns. "Our cousins are shedding their winter coats."

"Our cousins?"

"The deer." Paul took another few steps. "Here, look at this."

Faith found herself staring at the imprint of a cloven hoof in the earth. "That's from a deer?" she asked.

"Yes. The deer like to spend the night in a pine grove just past those blackberry vines over there." He pointed off to his right. "The pines keep out the wind."

"Okay, then what?"

"Then what?"

"What's the trail about?"

Paul blinked twice as he absorbed the question, and then waved his arm in a vague circle. "The deer have to drink and get food. They can't just walk in a straight line. There's a swampy area over there and a patch of blackberries and raspberries they could never get through. Over here, you've got fallen trees and the ground is covered with brush and fallen branches. The deer have been using the same trails for...I guess near forever. Other animals use the trail, too. Raccoons and possums and rabbits. It's just an easy way to get around."

"And that's how you find your way through the woods? By memorizing the trails?"

Paul Crow finally smiled. "Exactly." He turned and started off. "Come, I'll show you."

After a few minutes of easy going, Faith was able to follow the trail as it wound around various obstacles, until they finally came to a patch of shrubs bearing masses of waxy white flowers. To Faith, the flowers resembled lily of the valley, but lily of the valley grew close to the ground and the shrubs were higher than her head.

"What's..."

Paul put his fingers to his lips before whispering into Faith's ear: "Blueberries." Then he dropped to his knees and crawled in between two of the bushes.

At first Faith was put off by the boy getting so close to her. But as she followed anyway, she heard the sound of galloping hooves. She assumed they were deer, but there was no sign of life when they emerged into an open marshy patch of ground. There were no tall trees in the marsh and the newly sprouted reeds and grasses were so green in the sunlight that Faith closed her eyes for a moment.

She understood, without being told, why the deer sought out this spot. After a long winter, the young plants in the clearing were a feast for the gods, maybe even *Mesingwe* himself.

"I scared the deer off, right?" she said. "Because I was so loud."

"That's okay. The deer are too thin yet to hunt and the fawns have just been born."

"But I was too loud."

"You can't sneak up on deer," Paul explained. "Most of the time, the People lie in wait for the deer to come along."

"And what about the rest of the time?"

"The rest of the time we run them down." Paul started back through the blueberry shrubs. "Deer can run very fast," he called over his shoulder, "but men can run very far."

"What about women?"

"Women don't hunt."

Faith was still annoyed by Paul's dismissive response—talk about a hard-and-fast rule—when they suddenly broke through an especially tight cluster of maple saplings to find themselves on a rocky outcropping at the edge of the forest. They were standing a few yards from the top of a sheer cliff, a thousand feet above an immense valley, and the view of towns and farms and stretches of forest was stunning. In the far distance, the Delaware River was a thin blue line backed by the steep rise of a mountain range lost in haze. Above them, the sky was bright blue and the drifting clouds glowed at the edges. A flock of geese, their wings beating furiously, formed a long wedge only a few hundred feet away. Below the geese, a soaring hawk turned in slow circles, its translucent red tail feathers seeming almost afire.

Paul sat on the bare rock and folded his legs, one over the other. Faith followed suit. She dropped to her knees then sat back with her legs in front of her, content to allow the silence to build.

And so they remained, side by side, staring into the great distance, until Paul finally spoke his mind and Faith understood why he'd brought her to this place.
"Once the People roamed free over all this land. No man claimed ownership and no law allowed one man to own thousands of acres while another owned nothing. In the spring, all the clans gathered by the river to capture the millions of shad and alewives as they swam upstream to spawn in the little creeks. This was a happy time for the People. They stayed in camp until the run ended, catching and drying the fish, throwing one feast after another. The old stories were told, and the People danced and sang from sunset to dawn. Now, all of the land along the river is owned by someone. You need a permit to drop a fishing line into the water, but even that doesn't really matter. The fish are mostly gone, trapped a hundred years ago by white men at the mouth of the river."
Faith didn't know what to say and so she said nothing. After all, she was one of the white people about whom he was speaking, though Paul didn't seem to recognize that. Maybe because she wasn't one of the "white *men*," he didn't hold her accountable. In fact, because she was a female, maybe he didn't count her at all.
But then Paul looked at her—without bitterness, his expression neither more nor less grave than before—and she felt she had to say something.
"Tell me about the spirits that Indians believe in."
Before them, the red-tailed hawk called once, a single piercing note that seemed, in its own way, as lonely as the

call of the loon. Paul looked up hopefully, but quickly settled down.

"Every man needs a spirit guide, his *nianque*," he said. "Finding your spirit guide is..."

"*Nianque*? What's that?"

"Oh, I forgot for a moment." Paul finally smiled. "A *nianque* is an animal spirit that guides you when you have to make difficult decisions. Guides you throughout your life."

"That's good, right?"

"It is, but a spirit guide isn't some kind of gift. You have to find your *nianque*. That means going into the forest by yourself and staying there until the journey is completed. No matter how long it takes."

"Have you found your...*nianque*?"

"No, I have to wait a couple of years. I'm too young now."

"But you're going to try?"

"How can a man live his life without a guide? How would he find his way among the spirits that sow confusion?"

"You keep talking about men." Faith shook her head. "What about women? Do women get spirits to guide them?"

"Sometimes, if the spirit comes to them. Then they became very powerful."

Faith hesitated, powerful women being a somewhat new idea to her. In the city, only very poor women had jobs. They worked in horrible factories for next to nothing. Women of her class were expected to raise the children and take care of the home. Men had all the real power.

"Do you know why the People in our village don't own dogs?" Paul asked.

"I have no idea."

"Because the white man says we have to keep dogs chained, otherwise they might hunt the deer that white men want to hunt in the fall. In the old days, no Indian could tell another Indian what to do. Not even the most powerful chief. The People lived free and each man spoke for himself. Now the law tells us when we can hunt and when we can fish. In the spring, the People used to catch some of the geese and ducks as they passed through on their journey to the Grandfather Who Lives in the Cold. Now they tell us we can only catch birds in the fall. Once a man built a house for his family wherever he chose. Now they tell us where to build and put a tax on every home."

Paul turned to stare at the moving shadows cast by the clouds overhead. He didn't turn back when he finally chose to speak, aiming his words into the void.

"My parents may live among the People," he said, "but they work for Jaspin Gore. My father is the groundskeeper. He works from spring until the first snowfall. My mother is an all around housekeeper. She only works when Gore and his daughter use the house."

"So, what's wrong with that? We're in a Depression. They're lucky to have jobs."

Faith paused for a response that never came. Instead, Paul rose to his feet and led her back into the forest, back into his world.

Nine

THEY WENT FISHING late in the afternoon, using worms as bait, the biggest and fattest Paul could dig out of the compost heap. Faith Covington didn't touch the worms, of course, nor was she particularly thrilled to watch Paul bait the hooks later on. But the lake, when Paul finally pushed the canoe into the water and hopped onto the back, graceful as cat, was truly beautiful. The sun was dropping in the west and its dazzling light shot across the rolling waters, a pathway of molten gold suitable for royalty. Or for one of Paul Crow's many spirits.

Faith sat in front, facing forward, while Paul propelled the wooden canoe with a long paddle. Paul had promised to teach her to paddle, but there wasn't enough time before dinner to both teach and fish. Now Faith, her eyes sweeping across the waters as she scanned the lakefront and found no trace of another home, felt a calm settle over her. To her right, a flock of small birds, perhaps fifty, bobbed on the waters. The birds had snow-white bodies and jet-black wings. Their heads were black in front and white in back. As if their Creator couldn't make up His mind.

"What are they called?" Faith's right arm traced a half-circle that set the canoe rocking. She yanked her arm back and froze. According to Ben, there was still ice on the lake a few weeks ago. Falling in would do her no good at all. Maybe that's why Paul was steering a course that kept them close to shore.

"Buffleheads."

Buffleheads? Was he mocking her? "And what about those?" Faith pointed, this time more carefully, to another black-and-white duck. This duck's head was almost totally black.

"Golden-eyes."

This Faith could accept. The small bird did, indeed, have an eye the color of gold. She pointed to a third black-and-white bird, this one much larger, with a totally black head and a sharply pointed bill. The animal was swimming very low in the water and the single eye it turned to Faith was fiery orange.

"And that one?"

"That's a loon. They say that loons speak for the dead."

Paul was about to add something when the loon slid beneath the surface without stirring up as much as a ripple. Faith kept her eyes riveted to the spot where the bird disappeared, expecting it to reappear close to where it went down. But the loon didn't come up for nearly a minute and when its head finally broke the surface, unleashing a little fountain of sun-bright water, it was at least fifty yards from the canoe.

"What was the loon doing underwater?" Faith asked.

"Fishing, which we better get to."

They were abreast of a small projection of land when Paul tossed an anchor into the water and baited the hooks on his and Faith's fishing rods. "Do you see where those reeds start?" he asked.

Faith nodded. The growing reeds shooting up from the lake marked the boundary of deep and shallow water, that much was obvious.

"The big fish live in the open water," Paul continued. "The little fish live in the reeds where the big fish can't get to them. We want to put our hooks on the boundary."

He demonstrated by flipping the line out to within inches of the reeds. Then he handed the fishing rod to Faith. "Now, when you get a bite, make sure you keep the tip of the rod high in the air. Let the fish run for a few seconds until it gets tired then give..."

Paul didn't have a chance to complete his instructions. Faith's line exploded, running out so fast that the spinning reel whined like an animal in pain. Instinctively, Faith clamped down on the rod's long handle. Just as well, because the living, fighting animal on the other end of the line would have surely yanked the rod out of her hands if she hadn't. From a distance, she heard Paul repeat his earlier instructions: "Keep the tip up." But Faith's mind only had room for the vibrating fishing rod and for the life at the end of the line. The fish swam out into the lake for fifty yards before doubling back then suddenly leaped into the air, its writhing silver body flashing in the sunlight.

Faith didn't panic, though she knew that even a few weeks before she probably would have. The stark reality of an animal fighting for its life was now overwhelming. There was no evading the fact. Slowly, when the fish came to a stop, she began to spin the handle on the reel, drawing the animal toward the canoe. The panicked fish swam again, this time breaching the surface of the lake three times before it slowed.

"Give the rod a little yank," Paul said. "To set the hook."

Faith did as she was told, responding to Paul's calm tone. The fish appeared to be spent, its efforts to escape now feeble. Faith reeled it in easily. Behind her, she heard Paul's voice, but the words were unintelligible. The fish was within a foot of the canoe and Paul was leaning over the side, careful to maintain his balance while he reached for the end of the line.

"What did you say?" Faith asked.

"I was thanking *Mesingwe* for this gift. I was telling him how sorry I am to be taking one of his animals and that I would pray for the spirit of the fish to pass over. I told *Mesingwe* that tonight I would leave his offering in the fire."

Faith knew her Bible well enough to be familiar with the old saying: "Pride goeth before a fall." She even knew that Proverbs was being misquoted in that expression. "Pride goeth before destruction, and a haughty spirit before a fall." That was the way it really went. What it meant was not to get too full of yourself or something could happen that would cut you down to size.

None of that mattered, however, when she proudly carried the four largemouth bass (cleaned, of course, by Paul Crow) to her mother. For the first time in her young life, Faith felt that she'd contributed to the family. Not just by cleaning her room or making her bed, but in an actual, material way. She didn't even feel guilty about the fish, though they were the first living things she had killed, besides swatting a few pesky flies or mosquitoes here and there.

As Faith watched her mother coat the fish with corn meal and drop them into a hot frying pan, she realized that the work she'd done in the garden that morning had also contributed. When her mother had informed her that everyone worked on the farm, she'd imagined herself a drudge, her chores forced upon her. She had a better understanding of the Indian philosophy now. Everyone worked because everyone had to work. There just wasn't enough extra to support a life of leisure.

Faith's pride was further enhanced by Aunt Eva's two guests, Paul Crow and an elderly man named Elvin Red-Moon. Both seemed grateful for this addition to a meal of what Aunt Eva called "greens and beans." Faith, herself, was grateful. She'd eaten fish in the past, but never fish just taken from her own lake. The tender flesh slipped off the bone as though attracted to her fork by some kind of magnetism.

The first piece of fish was put back in the fire, an offering to *Mesingwe*. But the second was placed before Faith. As she'd caught all four of the fish, she was entitled to the first portion. Not that her piece was bigger than anyone else's. Sharing was what the People did, according to Red-Moon, who seemed to be some sort of tribal elder. Bragging rights, on the other hand, were another matter. Faith had provided for the community and her contribution was formally acknowledged. That done, she was promptly ignored.

The conversation at dinner, and over coffee afterwards, once again centered on Scranton Properties and its determination to drive the People away from Wildwood Lake. This wouldn't be a problem, all agreed, if the People were united, but they weren't. Already, two families had moved off the mountain. Now a second faction, led by a man named Caleb Littlewolf, was threatening to bolt as well.

Neither Aunt Eva nor Red-Moon, as all called him, intended to move. Their concern was for the People. True, their community was tiny by American standards. But that didn't bother Eva Darkcloud Benton.

"We've been kicked from pillar to post for three hundred years. When does it end? Where does it end? Red-Moon, your parents came here in the 1840s, nearly one hundred years ago, and this is where you want to end your days. By what right are you to be forced out?"

Tall and slender, Elvin Red-Moon had a warm smile, a smile echoed in a pair of lime-green eyes made all the more startling by his dark skin. He was smiling when he responded to Aunt Eva.

"Forced out? No one's used force." His voice was slow and even.

"Not yet, but it's coming."

"How do you know that?"

"Because that's the way it works, going all the way back to when the Dutch bought Manhattan from the People for a box of trinkets. Do you really believe the Canarsee wanted to sell their land? Because, to my way of thinking, the message was plain: Take the trinkets or we'll seize the land and you'll get nothing."

Margaret leaned over and whispered in her daughter's ear. "The Canarsee were a Lenape tribe who lived in Brooklyn. They only came to what the People called Mannahatta in the summer."

Faith nodded. The controversy had her attention, for sure, but the stakes didn't mean as much to her. She wasn't an Indian and wasn't about to become one. Not so Paul, who hung on every word. To Faith, who was watching, Red-Moon and Paul appeared to have a special relationship. Maybe that was because Paul's folks worked for Jaspin Gore while Red-Moon lived independently, despite his age. Faith estimated Red-Moon to be around eighty years old. A lifetime spent in the sun had cut deep creases in his cheeks and around his mouth, but he nevertheless sat straight in his chair and his broad chest seemed untouched by time.

Later on, when they were alone, Faith asked Aunt Eva if Paul and Red-Moon were related. Aunt Eva and Faith had volunteered to clean up so Margaret could write a letter to her husband. Faith planned to add a paragraph of her own before she went to sleep.

"No, they're not, but they're as close as two peas in pod. See, in the old days, the People lived most of their lives outdoors. Everyone knew everyone else and it was pretty common for a child to choose an adult outside the family as a guide. Red-Moon is a proven warrior; he won a Medal of Honor in the Great War. Paul's father, on the other hand, is a good man, a man who works hard to provide for his family. But his way is not the way of the People. He is not a warrior and he doesn't want to be one."

"What is his way?"

"To buy his groceries at the grocery store. To have an electric stove and heat in the house and a radio in his parlor."

Faith grabbed a clean dish towel and dried the plate in her hand. She laid the plate atop a stack on the shelf. "Is there something wrong with that?"

"Like I told you before, Indians don't tell other Indians what to do. Judson Crow has to make his own choices, and so does Winona Crow."

"And Paul, too?"

"That's right. Paul has to make his own choices and for now he's chosen the Indian way. But keep in mind, honey, Paul's only twelve years old. A few years from now, he may change his mind."

Faith found the answer entirely acceptable and went back to work. She had another question she was dying to ask; the words had been on the tip of her tongue for hours. Still, she waited until the dishes were washed and put away before she asked it.

"Aunt Eva?"

Aunt Eva gave Faith a sideways glance. Something important was coming. "Yes, honey?"

"Do you have a spirit guide?"

"Ah, you and Paul have done some talkin'. That's good. And, yes, I do. You understand, the People don't talk much about their guides. What goes on between an Indian and her guide is personal."

"Okay, but Paul told me that women with spirit guides are very powerful. Are you powerful?"

Aunt Eva laughed until she had to grab her sides, until Faith began to laugh along with her. When both quieted, Aunt Eva finally spoke. "Do you remember what Elvin Red-Moon said about the spirits and the Europeans?"

Faith did remember Red-Moon's little speech. At the time, she'd suspected him of directing it at her.

"When the Europeans came here with their guns and their diseases and their barrels of rum," he'd said, "don't you think we prayed to our spirits? Don't you think we asked the Great Father to protect us? The priests among us surely went to the spirit world for help, and the People surely made every sacrifice. The warriors among us had their say, too, and we went to war many times, until the people were driven further and further west, until they could fight no more."

Aunt Eva cleared her throat and Faith looked up. "The funny part is I rely on my guide even more than if I lived in the old days. Now that the teachings are mostly gone, and you can't tell a Lenape ceremony from a Mohawk ceremony, I speak with my guide almost from minute to minute."

An hour later, Faith lay in her bed, listening to the patter of rain on the roof and in the yard outside her window. From time to time, the steady drumming of the rain was penetrated by the cry of a distant loon and by an owl perched much closer to the house. It was amazing to her that she could already recognize the sounds of the different animals.

Faith was thinking about her mother and father. Margaret had grown very quiet since they'd gotten there. She went about her chores without complaining and didn't object even to Faith going out in the canoe. That was way out of character.

About her father, Faith didn't have a clue and she compensated by trying to imagine him with them on the lake. What would he think of Aunt Eva? Would he laugh at the way she gardened? Thomas Covington had worked with some of the most progressive and efficient corporations in New York. Not Aunt Eva. Aunt Eva had her shoulder pressed against the wheel of progress. She wanted to preserve a way of life that by her own admission was already lost.

Outside, the rain picked up and a gusting wind set the window glass to rattling in its frame. The owl cried again and again—*hoo, hoo, hooooooo*—its cry blending with the howl of the wind and the pounding rain until Faith imagined all to come from a single animal, a creature outside the boundaries that separate the things of the earth. Only the walls of the house kept this creature at bay.

Ten

OVER THE NEXT few weeks, Faith Covington tried to settle into what Aunt Eva called the Indian way of life. Faith had no other choice, since no other way of life was likely to present itself while she lived on her Aunt Eva's farm. Fortunately, she found this new little universe fascinating, if a bit taxing.

First of all, she and Aunt Eva, working together in the mornings, finished planting corn in only a few days. For the next couple of weeks, until the corn sprouted, there was nothing more to do.

But, no, that wasn't right. There was no more work to do in the garden, so Aunt Eva took Faith on long outings in the forest, where they gathered the leaves of wood sorrel, colt's foot, trillium, wintercress, and wild mustard, and the tubers of water lilies and spatterdock and Indian cucumbers and swamp potatoes. Wild onion and wild ginger added spice to the cooking; Aunt Eva harvested both wherever she found them—with Faith's help, of course.

The work was hard—not only the long walks, but the digging as well. The forest floor was a tangle of roots, some as thick as Faith's wrist, others as thin as a hair. The spade they hauled through the woods, the spade that had slid so easily into the compost heap, barely penetrated the soil. Plus, whoever wielded the shovel had to be careful not to cut the roots and tubers they were trying to harvest. And if a particular plant grew in a swampy area, the work was even more demanding.

For the first few days, it was all Faith could do to keep up. Everything was new, from the plants to the trails and streams Aunt Eva so easily followed. Still, Faith continued to analyze the basic question she'd asked on the first day: Was it worth it? All this work and they never seemed to gather more than enough for the night's meal. What would happen if Aunt Eva got sick? Would Ben make up the difference? From what Faith could see, Ben kept the house and the outbuildings in good repair, and fished from time to time, and that was it.

To Faith's credit, she waited until the fourth day, a Saturday, to put the question to Aunt Eva. "Is your way of life, with all its uncertainties, worth the effort?"

To Aunt Eva's credit, she didn't hesitate to answer. Nor was her answer condescending. She spoke plainly to her young grandniece, one adult to another.

"I don't mean to hurt you," Aunt Eva said, "but it seems to me the white man's way hasn't done all that much for you and your family. Yes, you lived well, and for a long time. I admit that. But then the economy fell on top of you, like a tree hit by lightning. Here, the forest provides food for humans and animals alike. And the forest is dependable, Faith. Not like the white man's economy, where one day you're on top of the world, the next you're broke."

FINDING FAITH

Faith watched Aunt Eva trace the root of a swamp potato, following its length to a round tuber on the end. She cut off this bulb with a paring knife and placed it in her basket. Then she pointed to a spot a foot away and signaled Faith to dig again.

"I'm not sayin' it's all roses," Aunt Eva said. "Springtime is hard, Lord knows, especially with the law telling us when and what and where we can hunt. Most of the money from the tourists is gone by spring, so it's all I can do, come April and May, to buy coffee and put gas in the truck. But life gets easier as the season goes along. There are pin-cherries and choke-cherries already past blooming, and blackberries thick enough in August to pick by the quart, and nuts to gather in the fall, and all manner of game to hunt."

"I don't know, Aunt Eva. I'm starting to think I'd rather be rich." Faith spoke her mind, the way she usually did around her aunt. "Maybe I'll find a rich husband. The Depression can't last forever."

"A rich husband?" Aunt Eva snorted. "In the old days, matters between husbands and wives were more or less on an equal footing."

"Are you—"

Although the owl made not a sound as it settled onto a branch of a towering elm tree, Faith was momentarily distracted by the flurry of wings. She watched the bird's head turn to the right, revolving three-quarters of the way around, watched it come back until the animal's butter-yellow eyes stared into hers.

"Does the owl think I'm food?" she asked Aunt Eva.

"No, most likely it's lookin' at us because we're a threat. Folks sometimes kill owls for their feathers."

"Then why doesn't it fly away, if it's afraid of us?"

Aunt Eva laughed, even as she shook her head. "Girl, do I look like a bird? Do I look like I have a bird's brain?

Now, go on, put some weight behind that shovel. We got a right far way to go before supper."

When she wasn't with Aunt Eva, Faith passed much of the time with Paul, who refused to gather roots—that was a woman's job. They were either in the forest or on the lake. Paul taught Faith how to paddle a canoe, and how a canoe is made. The one they were using had been constructed from a cedar log by Ben Hightower years before. He'd begun with the log itself, building a small fire across the top, chopping out a few inches of burned wood, then setting another fire, on and on and on, until the wood was thin enough to use on the lake.

The job had taken months to complete and the finished canoe was much heavier than canoes made in factories—much heavier and virtually indestructible. Paul and Faith caught any number of fish from inside it, while Ben fished from shore. This was no pastime, as Faith learned on Friday, when they caught no fish at all. They would have had to settle for greens and beans and corn bread if Paul hadn't shot a woodchuck trying to sneak into Aunt Eva's garden. By that time, Faith knew the gun Paul carried wasn't a rifle, but a twenty-gauge shotgun suitable only for smaller animals.

Ben cooked the woodchuck over an outdoor fire, turning it on a spit. The first morsel, naturally, was tossed into the fire, and the second went to Paul. Not that there was much for anyone, or that Faith relished the idea of eating a creature that lived in a hole underground. But after a day in the forest, she was way too hungry to be particular. She ate the meat on her plate, the beans and the greens, the corn bread and two cookies made with beech nuts and blackberry preserves. Only then, with Paul gone home and Ben retired to his room, did Faith return to the conversation interrupted by the owl's sudden appearance.

"What you said today, Aunt Eva, about husbands and wives living on an equal basis? Tell me what you meant."

Aunt Eva glanced at Margaret, who was standing by the sink, but Margaret kept her eyes down.

"Among the People, men and women had different jobs to do," Aunt Eva explained. "Women cared for the babies. They gathered food, the way you and me been doin'. They also cooked and sewed clothes for the winter and made the pottery. Men built the houses and did the hunting and most of the fishing, and they protected the People from some of the other tribes."

Faith rose to her feet. She picked up her plate and carried it to the sink. "What does that have to do with husbands and wives being equal?"

"Patience, girl, I'm gettin' to that. First thing, the People were divided in three clans—turtle, wolf, and turkey—and you couldn't marry someone in your own clan. When folks did get married, the husband came to live in his wife's clan. He was expected to build a house for her and their children, and to provide for the table. If the marriage broke up, which marriages had a habit of doin' even back then, the wife kept the house and everything in it, including the children, who had to be raised by her clan. There was no takin' the kids and leavin' a woman with nothing."

Faith was about to respond when Margaret spun around. "Don't be filling my daughter's head with nonsense, Aunt Eva. The truth is that when a man died, his widow was given to his brother as a second wife. And that's because a woman couldn't survive without a man."

"And a man couldn't survive without a woman," Aunt Eva shot back. "Someone had to care for the children while the men were away hunting. Someone had to dig roots and pick berries and gather nuts and plant the gardens. And that's the whole point, Margaret. Everybody contributed and no man could claim to be the sole support of his family."

That night, Faith stood by her bedroom window, as she had on the night before and the night before that. A swelling moon, surrounded by millions upon millions of stars, shone from the center of the sky, and it seemed to Faith as if those stars had come out only to pay homage to the moon's majesty. According to Paul, the moon was a spirit, one of the *manetuwaks*, whose job it was to keep the People safe at night. Personally, when it came to safety at night, Faith preferred walls.

The need for safety, from walls or moon, became apparent only a few seconds later when a movement at the edge of Faith's vision—a great shaggy shadow—drew her attention. Then another moment passed, a moment of confusion, before her brain admitted that she was looking at a very large bear.

The animal ambled past the house, hugging the edge of the forest, in no apparent hurry. It stood once to sniff the air, its black head rising above the height of the window, its dark eyes so small as to be nearly invisible. Then it dropped to all fours and disappeared behind a poplar tree at the far end of the yard.

Hoo, hoo, hooooooo.

Faith smiled with relief as she raised her eyes to the owl on its perch in the poplar's upper branches. The pale moonlight fell across its feathers, making them seem even more like a robe, and Faith briefly imagined the animal in some ancient court, an advisor to Cleopatra or the Queen of Sheba.

Paul Crow was nervous around owls. He believed they were messengers of change, and not always for the better. Personally, Faith had a hard time imagining a change worse than the ones she'd already been through. She was becoming more and more attached to the bird. When the owl finally stopped coming around, as it surely would, she knew she would miss it.

"Faith?"

Faith turned to find her mother sitting up in bed. "Yes?" she asked.

"Is something wrong?"

The question annoyed Faith. Whenever she did anything different, her mother assumed that something was wrong. Her reaction was a mystery. Why would a mother encourage her daughter to be independent, yet become instantly panicked when she acted independently?

Wisely, Faith kept those thoughts to herself. "No," she said, "I just like to look out the window at night. There was a bear in the yard a minute ago."

Margaret rose from the bed, slipped into a robe, and joined her daughter. The owl took that moment to hoot again.

"That owl..." Margaret said, shaking her head. "He gives me the creeps."

"How do you know it's a he? Why not a she?"

"You've been listening to Aunt Eva. But you're right, the owl could be female." Margaret hesitated, and then said, "How are you doing, baby? I know all this must be hard for you."

"I feel completely isolated. You know, being here without a telephone? I want to speak to Daddy, but he seems very far away. It's like I walked through a door into a new world and now I can't find my way out." Faith paused then continued. "Only it's not a horrible world, not at all. I never would have thought that I could do the things I do now. But I can. I can put a worm on a hook and I can clean a fish. I can dig in the garden and in the woods. I'm even starting to find my way around in the forest."

"Don't tell me you're becoming an Indian. I have enough to worry about."

"No, not an Indian. But something, Mom. Something I wasn't before."

Eleven

THE NEXT MORNING, after Faith Covington and Margaret took turns bathing in water heated on the stove, the family went to church in Pocono Summit. Faith, naturally, donned a dress for the occasion, a dress and her best patent leather shoes. Then she brushed the tangles out of her hair before checking herself in the bathroom mirror. Though all was well with her appearance, she felt oddly conspicuous, as if she'd put on a costume.

A question rose into her consciousness as she stared at her reflection, a question she'd never before asked herself: Who am I?

Her mother called out before Faith provided an answer. "Faith, Red-Moon's here. We need to get moving."

The pickup's cab being too small to hold four people in Sunday clothes, Margaret and Faith rode to church in Elvin Red-Moon's 1924 Buick. A luxury car on the day it was first purchased, ten years prior, the Buick had fallen on hard times. The car's red paint was faded, its leather upholstery worn smooth, and some loose part in the undercarriage banged every time they hit a pothole. But the Buick was clean, inside and out, and Faith wasn't all that interested in the ride anyway. According to Paul Crow, Red-Moon was more committed to the old religion, to the religion of the People, than anyone in the community. So much so that some believed him to be a *shaman*. But, then, why did he attend a Christian church every Sunday? Why, in winter, if he believed the world to be run by spirits, did he trudge a half-mile on snowshoes just to get to his car?

"Mr. Red-Moon..."

"*Mister?* Please, Miss Faith, it's just Red-Moon. Or Elvin, if it suits you better."

"Alright, then. I have a question I want to ask you. Paul told me that you believe in the spirits. You know, the old religion."

"Okay."

"Well, I want to know why you go to a Christian church."

"You want to know how I can believe in God if I believe in the *manetuwak*?"

"If the *manetuwaks* are the spirits, then yes."

Red-Moon chuckled. "Did you know that the People believed in a single creator *before* the white man arrived, just like Christians and Jews?"

"No, I didn't."

"Well, they did, and his name is *Kishelemukong*. He created the heavens and earth and everything in between." Red-Moon winked at Faith. "So far, so good, right?"

Faith smiled. Red-Moon's humor was infectious. Unlike Paul Crow, who took everything seriously, Red-Moon was always smiling.

"Right," she said.

"Well, unfortunately, *Kishelemukong* decided to ignore his creation once it was complete. So he turned over the job of maintaining the creation to the *manetuwak* and got on with his business. That's why Jesus is so important. Jesus is the link, the Son of the Creator who remembered His creation. As for the spirits... How many people are on their knees right now, asking saints or angels for help? And what about devils? *Mahtantu* is an evil spirit who exists only to plague human beings. Now, if you want to say that the Archangel Gabriel is real and *Muxumsa Wapanewank*, who rules over the winds, is a myth, that's fine with me. I don't expect everything to fit into place, all neat like a picture puzzle. I just know what lives in my heart."

Faith didn't really know what Red-Moon was saying, not in her head. But in a way, something inside her understood.

At church, Faith was surprised to find young Pauline Gore sitting on a front row pew beside a middle-aged man. The man wore a tweed jacket with leather patches on the elbows, though the day was rapidly warming. A thick gold watch circled his right wrist and he sported a long gray mustache that curled up at the edges.

"Who's that?" Faith whispered to her mother.

"Jaspin Gore."

Red-Moon, Margaret, and Faith took seats toward the back of the little church. They were soon joined by Ben and Aunt Eva. Then Paul Crow arrived, accompanied by his parents, along with a number of other Indian families. They clustered together in the pews on the left side of the aisle. The white families, for the most part, sat on the right side. From time to time, Faith noticed that Paul stole sidelong glances at her. It occurred to Faith that Paul had never seen her in a dress before.

Reverend John Moore's sermon was heavy on trusting the Lord in these hard, hard times. Though Faith didn't fidget, this was old news to her. Every religious figure in the country preached on this theme. She was more interested in Aunt Eva and Ben. Even with all their talk of spirits, they offered the proper responses to the prayers, listened attentively to the lessons and the Gospel reading, and finally took part in the communion meal. Then, true to her word, Aunt Eva shook Reverend Moore's hand after the service ended, inquiring after his wife who'd been ill, without mentioning *Mesingwe* or any other spirit.

Faith remembered to be polite when she was introduced to Reverend Moore, but her attention was focused on Pauline, who emerged from inside the church holding her father's hand. Well over six feet tall, Jaspin Gore walked with a heavy stride, each foot planted firmly, as though he were claiming the space for all eternity. He led his daughter up to Reverend Moore and Aunt Eva, ignoring Faith and Margaret as he passed.

"Eva," he said. "Good morning."

Aunt Eva returned the greeting with a smile. "Jaspin."

And that was that. Jaspin Gore shook Reverend Moore's hand and led his daughter across the yard to his waiting Cadillac. No chauffeur this time. Jaspin opened the door and stepped back to let his daughter pass. Without a murmur, Pauline got into the front seat. Only when her father circled the car did she roll down the window to wave at Faith.

"Hi, Faith, I've got to go home now. We're having guests to dinner. Soooooo borrrrrring."

This time Faith wasn't fooled. Pauline Gore's blue eyes were wells of loneliness. Like Faith, she'd been yanked from her familiar surroundings in New York. Unlike Faith, she'd found no other life to replace the old one.

That afternoon, the entire community came together at Aunt Eva's little farm to hold a general council. Though each family brought food, the People were more interested in discussion than eating. Faith was struck by the intimacy (everyone knew everyone else) and by the lack of children. Except for the Crows, only two couples had children, and they were still in diapers. Most of the men and women were older, a few truly elderly.

Once the People got going, they couldn't stop. Every member was entitled to express an opinion, and to keep expressing it until the matter—whether or not to sell out—was resolved. Faith watched, fascinated, for the first hour. In the movies, Indians were always portrayed as strong, silent types. Not these Indians.

The discussion soon broke down along familiar lines. There were those, like Aunt Eva and Red-Moon, who considered their little farms to be an ancestral homeland. Pitiful, maybe, compared to the thousands of square miles they roamed in the past, but that was all they had. The opposition was led by a younger Indian named Caleb Littlewolf. In his early forties, Littlewolf was short and muscular. His face was dominated by a long, sharp nose that reminded Faith of her owl's hooked beak.

Caleb Littlewolf had come alone. He had no wife or children, and no great ties to the acreage he'd inherited only a few years before. Nevertheless, when he rose to speak, Littlewolf was eloquent.

"You claim this land to be the People's land," he said, addressing Elvin Red-Moon, "but you pay your property taxes to the government of Pennsylvania every year. By what right does the government of any state, or even the United States, demand property taxes from the People? Or from anyone else? The answer is very simple. The People don't own land and they never will. They rent land from the government."

Littlewolf went on for some time, illustrating the many ways a government could simply take land away—if the government wanted to build a school, for instance, or a road. True, the government was supposed to compensate landowners, but often that compensation was far from just, especially if you were an Indian. And compensation or not, landowners had no choice. They had to sell.

"I know we've been cheated many times in the past," he continued. "We gave away Manhattan and half of Pennsylvania for a handful of trinkets. We've been lied to and swindled and driven from our land by force. But not this time. The offers we've received from Scranton Properties are generous, much more than we could hope to get by selling our land on the open market, if we could sell it at all."

Aunt Eva was the next to speak. She looked around as she rose to her feet and stepped forward, her eyes bouncing from one face to another.

"Caleb's right, the offers are very generous. And that's just the problem. Here we are in the middle of a Depression and this company's goin' around buyin' up land that won't fetch a dollar an acre. Now I could understand if old Jaspin, or any of the other families, wanted to buy up the lakefront property. Someday it's gonna most likely be valuable. But that ain't the case, sisters and brothers. No, sir. Not one of us knows who owns Scranton Properties, or how they ever heard of us, or why they want the land. They got mysterious ways, and mysterious motives. Now, me, when I come on a mystery, I want to get to the bottom of it. Remember, it was gold that drove the Lakota out of the Black Hills."

As the arguments continued, Faith found herself drifting. She was sitting on a folding chair next to a makeshift table containing plates of food, including a pan of four baked chickens. Fresh sautéed bass was tasty enough, but after a week of fish chased with greens and beans, the oven-browned chickens looked very, very good.

Faith was reading a book, *Cimarron* by Edna Ferber, as she waited for the council to take a meal break. But the discussion went on and on, with no end in sight. Margaret was seated to Faith's left. She was mending the seam of a heavy quilt, which didn't make a lot of sense to Faith. Summer was on the way. The quilt wouldn't be needed again for months.

"Mom," Faith said quietly when she could no longer contain herself, "do Indians ever stop talking?"

"Not if they can help it." Margaret laid her sewing in her lap as she smiled up at her daughter. "Let me tell you a story. Once upon a time, nearly two hundred years ago, the People held a great council. All the chiefs attended, chiefs from every clan, chiefs from hundreds of miles away, from New York and New Jersey, from Pennsylvania and Delaware. They had a big decision to make, a very big decision, maybe the most important they would *ever* make. The council went on for a week, from dawn until well after dark, but they did eventually come to a consensus. And do you know what they decided?"

Faith shook her head.

"They decided to fight with the British in the Revolutionary War."

Twelve

AUNT EVA AND Faith Covington headed into the forest after breakfast the next morning, as they'd been doing for the past week. The paths Aunt Eva chose were becoming more familiar to Faith, at least for the first part of their hike. There was a patch of woodland marked by dozens of rounded gray rocks, all about the same height. Faith had come to call this formation the Graveyard. In another spot, a huge boulder, as high as Faith's little row house in New York City, rose above a marsh. A shrub grew from a crack in the boulder about halfway to the top, its roots somehow finding enough purchase to keep the plant from crashing to the ground. To Faith, the bush looked enough like a fat nose to earn a nickname: the Schnozz.

There was a stream as well, fairly wide and very slow running. Aunt Eva used this stream as a pathway almost every time they entered the forest, leading Faith along its banks, and occasionally over the rocks that marked its flow. Finally, there were the remains of dirt roads. No more than faint tracks, the roads—according to Aunt Eva—were constructed after the U.S. Civil War when every tree on the Pocono plateau had been cut down to provide fuel for the Lackawanna Railroad's steam engines.

They walked for almost an hour, until they finally reached a marshy clearing that included a small pond at the center. Faith and her aunt had come to harvest watercress, which grew in abundance here, but Faith's initial reaction had nothing to do with securing a meal. Here, in this hidden place, hundreds of blue irises had opened their blossoms to the sun. Their beauty, totally unexpected, brought her to a halt.

"Real pretty," Aunt Eva said. "I always look forward to comin' here."

"But they're irises."

"That's right. They're called blue flag."

Faith shook her head. "But they're irises," she repeated. "Irises grow in gardens."

"Not these. Unless the squirrels planted 'em. You think squirrels go in for gardenin'?" Aunt Eva's smile quickly faded. "Thing is, Faith, half the plants and bushes in the forest, includin' a hundred different flowers, were brought here by settlers."

"Why would they bring flowers to put in the woods?"

"They didn't, honey. The settlers hated the woods. What happened was the plants made seeds and the seeds escaped into the wild. Some of 'em, like blue flag, took a likin' to their new home. These flowers sprout up almost every year."

"Almost?"

"Back about three years ago, we had a dry winter. There wasn't two inches of snow and this marsh was dry as dust come spring. The blue flag didn't grow up that year."

"But it grew the next year?"

"And every year since." Aunt Eva laid her bag on the ground. "These irises? They may look beautiful, but they're wild things, honey. And wild things know how to survive."

A commotion in the branches above their heads broke through the conversation. Faith heard a buzzing sound, like an insect but moving way too fast, and the tearing of leaves, followed an instant later by the unmistakable crack of rifle. Before she knew what was happening, Faith found herself lying flat on the ground, Aunt Eva on top of her.

"Hold off on that shootin', ya dang fool," Aunt Eva shouted. "There's people around. You hear me?"

"Yeah, I hear you." Fifty feet away, on the other side of the marsh, Crease Marron walked out of the forest. He carried a rifle in his left hand, the barrel pointed at the ground. "What are you doin' out here, Pocahontas?"

Aunt Eva rose to her feet and Faith quickly followed suit. Faith was furious, both for the scare and the slur. But Aunt Eva's expression was frozen in neutral, a really wise move when Faith stopped to think about it. Marron was the only one armed.

"You're huntin' out of season," Aunt Eva said.

"You gonna call the police on me?" Marron ran a finger along the scar on his cheek. "Somehow, that don't seem right, bein' as you injuns kill anything any time you want. But I forgot, it's all your land to begin with. Least until white people took it from ya."

Aunt Eva didn't speak, though her gaze remained steady, as though she was carefully measuring her words, and it was Marron who broke the silence.

"You two squaws get on outta here." He brought the barrel of the gun up until it pointed at the sky. His index finger was inside the trigger guard. "And don't you come back any time soon. This here is my happy hunting ground and I don't mean to share it."

"Is that right?" Aunt Eva's temper finally got the better of her. "Crease Marron, you're nothin' but a coward and a bully. I can still remember the time my boy, Teddy, sent you crawlin' home to your momma. Now I came here to pick watercress and I'm not goin' home empty-handed, so you can just go hunt somewhere else."

Marron took a step forward. His face had reddened and his scar was a white streak running from his ear to the corner of his mouth.

"You're on private property," he said.

"Not yours."

"Don't see what that's got to do with anythin'. I'm an officer of the law."

"More like a fool. Anyway, I don't have time to argue. I come a long way and I have to get back."

Aunt Eva took a white cloth from her bag, the remains of a tablecloth, and spread it on the ground. Then she took off her shoes, rolled up the cuffs of her overalls and stepped into the pond. Squatting down, she began to pluck the stems and leaves of a plant growing just beneath the surface of the water. The stems came up easily, roots and all. Aunt Eva took the time to cut off the roots with a paring knife before tossing the stems and leaves onto the sheet.

Faith watched Crease Marron watch Aunt Eva. She was afraid, naturally. In Faith's little world, the one she'd left behind, only policemen had guns. Marron was a kind of policeman, but his attitude was far from the respectful greeting Officer Murphy offered to her and her mother when they appeared together on his beat. Plus, she and Aunt Eva were out in the middle of nowhere. If Marron worked up the nerve to use that gun, who would know?

But there was something else, a little matter that cut through her understandable fear without entirely driving her fear away. An unarmed woman was defying a man with a gun. What's more, unlike Faith, Aunt Eva seemed more angry than afraid, as if she'd like nothing more than to smack Crease Marron right across his nasty mouth.

Marron began to shift his weight back and forth, from his left foot to his right. His mouth and eyes scrunched down until they were little more than straight lines running across his face. He couldn't be any angrier.

"Mark my words," he said, his voice tight with emotion, "your day is comin' soon."

Message delivered, Crease Marron spun on his heel and vanished into the forest. A moment later, as if celebrating a victory, a gray owl settled in the lower branches of a hickory tree and began to hoot.

"He shot at you?" Paul Crow asked. He and Faith were sitting on rocks fronting the waters of Wildwood Lake. Supper would be served in just a few minutes and Paul had arrived a half-hour before with a last-minute contribution—that porcupine he'd been hunting for the past week. Aunt Eva had been ecstatic. The porcupine's quills could be used to decorate the garments she made for her souvenir stand.

"No, I can't say that. The bullet went through the tree right above our heads, but maybe that deputy constable was only hunting."

"For what?"

"For squirrels? Or birds?"

"Not with a rifle, Faith. Rifles are for big game, like deer and bear, and they don't live in trees, either."

"Maybe he just has bad aim."

Paul got to his feet, snatched up a handful of stones and began to skip them across the lake. Faith rose to stand behind him. Wildwood Lake had changed in the short time she'd been living on its shore. Most of the waterfowl had moved on, the buffleheads and the golden-eyes and mergansers, leaving only the geese, the mallards, and a pair of loons who kept well away from people. But there were babies everywhere, ducklings and goslings. The ducklings swam in a line behind their mother, tiny balls of yellow fluff, peeping ceaselessly. Faith knew that the ducklings, if they meant to survive, would have to undertake the long southern migration in the fall, but right now that didn't seem possible. They couldn't have weighed more than a few ounces.

"See, it don't make sense, Faith," Paul said after a long silence. "Nobody hunts bear and deer in the spring. First, because this ain't the huntin' season. Second, because the animals are so skinny, they ain't worth eatin', not unless you're starvin'. Tell me where this happened."

"Where?" Faith shrugged. "Well, I know it was past the Graveyard, past the Schnozz." Paul looked at her with a bewildered expression. "Oh, sorry—I don't know for sure. Maybe a couple of miles from the end of the stream. We went to pick watercress from a pond and there were all these irises there."

Paul hurled another stone out over the lake. The wind was up and the surface of the lake choppy. Paul's stone caught the base of a little wave and sunk out of sight.

"Do you mean blue flag?"

"Right, that's what Aunt Eva called them."

"I've been where you're talking about. That's on Caleb Littlewolf's property."

"How do you know that?"

"My parents have a survey map. In the winter, I study up on it." Paul grabbed another handful of stones, but stopped suddenly. He pointed to a huge bird flying across the lake. The bird flew with its long, thin neck tucked back against its chest, the beating of its immense wings slow and regular.

"A great blue," Paul said.

"A great blue what?"

"A great blue heron."

Faith watched the heron glide in for a landing at the edge of the lake. For a time it stood upright and motionless, but then, suddenly, its long, sharp beak darted below the surface of the lake. The bird came up empty, shook off the water and began a slow stalk through the shallow waters.

Paul, though appearing as calm as ever, seemed out of sorts to Faith, who began to think she could read him better. She felt he was making a bigger deal out of the incident with Crease Marron than was necessary. He was acting upset. *Protective*, even. She wondered if it had anything to do with her.

"I think I'll go out to that pond with the blue flag after dinner," Paul announced. "Take a look around."

"In the dark? What will your parents say?"

"They won't be home until late, if they get home at all. Jaspin Gore has guests at the house."

"And they have to stay there all night?"

"What can I say, Faith? Gore expects his servants to serve."

Following breakfast the next morning, Aunt Eva took Faith into the barn for a pottery lesson. The Lenape had been using clay pots for hundreds of years before the Dutch established their colony in Manhattan, a little fact that Aunt Eva twice repeated. Using the old methods, Aunt Eva went on to explain, she always made a few pots to sell at her souvenir stand. Not very many, though, because they were too expensive for most tourists.

The powdered clay they were to use had been collected in the fall and dried during the winter. Now it rested in one of two barrels stacked against an outer wall.

"You got to temper the clay," Aunt Eva explained as she pulled the covers off the barrels, "else the pot'll break apart when you put it in the fire. I could use crushed rock if I wasn't too old and lazy to crush it by hand. But I am too old and lazy, so I'm gonna use sand instead, which me and Ben collected down by the Delaware River. The sand's in this other barrel."

Aunt Eva wheeled and dragged both barrels to the center of the barn. She used a scoop to first shovel clay into a tin bucket, then sand. A careful mixing followed, with Aunt Eva running the little particles through her hand several times before she was satisfied. Then she added water, pausing often to test the consistency of the mixture.

"You ever seen pots made before?" Aunt Eva's busy fingers didn't slow down when she asked the question.

"Yes, they taught pottery making at my school. I never took that class, but I remember seeing it done. The students used a pottery wheel that spun around."

"Well, the People didn't have pottery wheels. The People used a different method. Slower, true, but we got the job done."

Aunt Eva withdrew a small bit of clay and rolled it between her palms until it formed a skinny tube. Quickly, she curled the length of the tube into a spiral before placing the wet clay on a flat board.

"This is the base, this little bit. Now, watch what I do next before you give it a try." Aunt Eva spun another piece of clay between her palms, but this time curled it around the spiral on the board. She pinched the two bits together, very carefully, until they were joined. "See, this is the tricky part. If you don't pinch 'em together just right, the pot's gonna crack when you put it in the fire and all your work's for nothin'. Now—"

That was as far as Aunt Eva got before the sound of an approaching car, the hum of the engine, and the crunch of wheels on the dirt road, brought her to a halt. Aunt Eva hesitated, waiting for the car to pass, but when the car stopped instead, she got to her feet and walked into the yard.

Faith followed, emerging into the daylight to find Crease Marron standing with an older man beside a black Oldsmobile. The older man was broad through the chest, but even wider through the belly. He wore suspenders instead of a belt and a broad-brimmed hat that had seen better days. A metal star pinned to his breast pocket gleamed dully.

"Mornin', Abe," Aunt Eva said.

Faith nodded to herself. This was Constable Abe Hoskins, the man who'd remained in the car while his deputy, Crease Marron, tormented Ben on that first day she arrived. In his own way, Hoskins was more threatening than Marron. He gazed at Aunt Eva through dark brown eyes devoid of emotion and his right hand rested at his waist, just a few inches above a holstered revolver that flapped against his hip. Marron, too, carried a gun—a revolver, but his was tucked into a holster strapped to his thigh. And that was another reason for Faith to dislike the deputy. Marron was trying to make an impression. He was playing the part of gunslinger in a western movie. Abe Hoskins, when it came to making an impression, didn't need to try. With him, the weapon spoke for itself.

"Eva." Hoskins came within a few yards of Aunt Eva before he stopped. Then he nodded to Margaret, who'd come out of the house. Faith, who was standing behind Aunt Eva, was ignored.

"State your business, Abe. I'm in the middle of my pottery makin' and I don't want that clay to dry."

"Eva, you've become downright rude. I can remember when you were more hospitable."

"I can remember when you were one of the People." Aunt Eva's eyes narrowed. "Like your mother."

Crease Marron chose that moment to make his presence known. "The People..."

"Shut up, Crease." Hoskins shifted his weight. "My mother's got nothin' to do with this," he told Aunt Eva.

"Your mother lived in the Indian way."

"And she died in the Indian way, too, from a pneumonia she never would have gotten if she lived in a house with real heat. And when she died, she didn't have enough money to put herself in the ground. I had to sell her house to pay for her funeral. If that's your fool Indian way, you can keep it."

From across the yard, Margaret gestured for Faith to join her, but Faith pretended not to notice. She was intensely curious; a new window had opened, as they'd been opening ever since she left New York. But there was an air of potential violence that frightened her as well.

"State your business, Abe."

"I got a complaint about a poached deer, Eva. Man says Ben Hightower shot it yesterday afternoon."

"Ben was here yesterday."

"That so?"

"Yes, it is. And you know that, too. Nobody poaches deer in the spring. So you can stop playin' the white man's fool. What's your business here?"

Aunt Eva's sharp tone made one thing obvious: She wasn't intimidated. But it was Abe Hoskins and his deputy who had the guns and the badges. Faith took a step toward her mother, but then stopped.

"My informant tells me that deer is hangin' in your barn right now," Hoskins said, "and I mean to search it."

"You got a warrant?"

"Nope."

Ben Hightower chose that moment to make an appearance. He came around the side of the house furthest from Hoskins and Marron. Ben was carrying a double-barreled shotgun. Not a small bird gun, like Paul's. Ben's shotgun looked big enough to take down a house.

"You ain't threatenin' an officer of the law, are you, Ben?" Hoskins asked. "'Cause that there would be a crime."

Ben didn't answer, but he didn't move, either. The barrel of the gun was pointed upward at a forty-five-degree angle and his finger was outside the trigger guard. He was merely waiting.

"Like I said," Hoskins shifted his gaze to Aunt Eva, "I mean to search your barn. Now move yourself out of the way, you and the brat."

"Now you're threatenin' children? That's what you come to, Abe Hoskins? Threatenin' children for a paycheck at the end of the week?"

"Eva, you need to get out of my way. Now."

Suddenly, Margaret Covington's voice broke through the tension. "Enough, Aunt Eva," she said. "That's enough."

The message was delivered with the same tone of exasperation Margaret often used on her daughter, and it was equally effective. Aunt Eva finally stepped aside, taking Faith with her.

"You wait here, Crease," Hoskins said as he ducked through the doorway. "And keep your mouth shut."

Aunt Eva trailed Hoskins into the barn, leaving Faith to watch from the doorway. Hoskins marched to the center of the barn's single room, to where Aunt Eva had been fashioning her pot. He looked down and shook his head.

"This the People's way?" he asked. "Pottery for tourists?"

"It was your momma who taught me how to make pots," Aunt Eva replied.

"That right?" Without asking permission, Hoskins walked to the far wall and opened one of a dozen boxes piled against it. He pulled out a gaudy headband with a dyed feather attached to the side. "How about this, Eva? My mother teach you this, too? Is this what she meant by the Indian way?" He pulled out a cheap cardboard drum with a few limp feathers tied to a strip of rawhide. "And this? This how the People lived? Sellin' trinkets to tourists?"

Hoskins stopped for a moment, but Aunt Eva remained silent. "Nothin' to say?" He picked up the box and read the address of the sender: "Ah-Ming Novelties, Hong Kong." He laughed. "But I guess it's all about maintainin' the old ways. Tell me somethin', Eva, do you do a little dance, maybe a war dance, for the tourists' benefit? I'm talking about a genuine, authentic war dance. Just like the People did back in the day when there was a People."

"And you, Abe Hoskins?" The voice belonged to Margaret and it cut across the little space, sharp as a knife. "When you put on that star, do you think the rich folks you work for mistake you for a white man? Because you've got Indian written all over your face, from your narrow eyes to the red in your cheeks. Yes, they'll let you do their dirty work, just like the French and the British used the People to do their dirty work nearly two hundred years ago. But you won't be invited to their table when the job is done. No, you'll still be an outsider. You'll always be an outsider."

Faith was amazed. Her mother's Indian past had never been mentioned in her presence. Obviously, the past was something her mother was trying to put to rest. But then Faith realized that Margaret Covington loved her Aunt Eva. And the simple fact that she'd chosen another way for herself made not a bit of difference. Family loyalty came first.

"You always did have a fresh mouth," Hoskins said to Margaret. "But I'm gonna overlook that, bein' as I have other things to do. Now, Eva, I got a message to deliver. Fact is, I been deliverin' it ever since I got here. You got to move out. If you move out, you and that stubborn old man you got for a neighbor, everyone else is gonna follow. So, I come to tell you that Scranton Properties is willing to increase their offer by half."

"I ain't motivated by money," Aunt Eva said at last. "Never have been."

"I told 'em you'd say that, but they asked me to come anyway." Hoskins took off his wide-brimmed hat and ran his fingers through his greasy hair. "They thought I could reason with you. But—"

The constable broke off in mid-sentence. He marched out of the barn, past Faith, past his deputy, who quickly followed, right up to the Olds. Then he turned to address Ben Hightower.

"You think the folk who want this land are afraid of that shotgun, Ben?"

"Can't say as I rightly know, bein' as I ain't give the matter a moment's thought. Can't say I rightly care, neither."

Abe Hoskins opened the door. He started to get inside, but then turned back to Ben. "You will," he said. "I can promise you that."

Thirteen

THAT NIGHT, FAITH Covington stood by the bedroom window for a long time. Constable Abe Hoskins and his curt warnings had taken up residence in her mind and she couldn't get them out. She needed to speak with someone, but not her mother, who had nothing to say beyond insisting that all this was about somebody wanting somebody else's land. Living in the old way, the Indian way, had nothing to do with it. The main point was the people who owned the land were poor and struggling while Scranton Properties' backers were wealthy and powerful. The landowners might be Irish or Italian or French—or anything else except rich enough to fight back—and the result would be the same.

Faith wanted to talk the whole business over with Paul Crow, but Paul hadn't come by that afternoon, nor had he shown up for supper. Another reason to worry. Then just before they sat down to their meal, Ben Hightower had returned from Pocono Summit with the mail, including a letter from Faith's father. The Federal Housing Administration, one of President Franklin Roosevelt's new agencies, had decided to locate a branch in Manhattan. They needed accountants, more than a dozen, and Thomas Covington had applied to be one of them. Of course, he was far from the only jobless accountant looking for a position with the FHA, so perhaps the opportunity would come to nothing. But he had an interview scheduled for the following afternoon and he was hoping for the best. The job paid a decent wage—not nearly as much as he was making before the Depression, but enough for them to live on.

There was other news, too. Sad news. The Covington's little house was gone, finally repossessed by the bank. Faith would never again live in the only home she'd ever known.

Faith stared across the yard at her owl. The night was overcast, with no moon to light the bird's feathers, and the owl now looked more like a monk than a minister in some royal court. Its yellow eyes were reduced to a pearly gray almost the same shade as its oddly sewn face.

On this night, the bird hadn't reacted when Faith's silhouette appeared in the window. The owl's beak was tucked beneath its left wing and it was digging away, preoccupied with some itch. Or so Faith guessed. She looked up at a gray sky cut by streaks of inky-black cloud that fell almost to the level of the treetops and wondered why her mother wasn't more concerned. Try as she might, Faith was unable to convince herself that Ben Hightower hadn't been ready to use that gun, or even that he'd been overly alarmed at the prospect of using it.

The owl lifted its beak and began to hoot. *Hoo, hoo, hooooooo.* Calling, waiting, calling again. According to Ben, Aunt Eva, and Paul, owls foretold a change in circumstances. But if that was so, Faith had to wonder what the animal was doing when the Great Depression—the source of every change in her life—began. In fact, her life wasn't about change, not anymore. The point was where those changes would take her. There was nothing false about Abe Hoskins, and no reason to believe his final threat was an empty one.

Faith turned away from the window and crossed the room to her mother's bed. Margaret Covington was sitting up, staring at her daughter.

"Mom, did I wake you?"

"Actually, that animal—that owl—woke me up." Margaret pushed a tendril of hair away from her face. "What about you?"

Faith ignored the question. "Why don't you look like an Indian?" she asked.

"What brought that up?"

"Well, if your mother was an Indian and your father was white, then you're half-Indian. But you don't look like Ben Hightower or Abe Hoskins or Caleb Littlewolf. Or even like Aunt Eva. Your hair isn't black and your eyes are more rounded than theirs. And even my hair is more blond than it is brown!"

"Honey, when I told you that your grandmother was Indian, I didn't mean to say... Look, both of grandma's parents called themselves Indian, but I know for a fact they had blood relatives who were white, and at least one Chinese ancestor who worked for the Union Pacific Railroad. But that's what I've been trying to tell you. Abe Hoskins is a nasty man, but he wasn't off the mark. And neither was Caleb Littlewolf. Aunt Eva's kidding herself. Taxes do have to be paid and that means tending a roadside tourist stand in the summer, smiling at the tourists, selling trinkets made in Hong Kong. This is not how the Lenape lived."

"But at least she's trying," Faith said.

"Maybe so, but the way she's pursuing is her own way, not the way of the People."

Faith smiled. "And what's wrong with that?" she asked.

Margaret was first to smell the smoke, which was odd because she was standing before the woodstove preparing breakfast. The stove was making its own smoke, of course, and that should have masked the piercing odor of Elvin Red-Moon's barn when it exploded into flame. It didn't. Margaret raised her head, sniffed the air and said, "Does anybody smell smoke?"

Aunt Eva was the first to react. She walked into the yard, looked around and then said calmly, "Ben, gather up the buckets."

Pocono Summit had a fire department, but Aunt Eva had no telephone to call them with. Not that it mattered. The firemen were all volunteers. They'd be at home or off to their regular jobs. Gathering them would take time, as would the drive from town. Unfortunately, fire didn't wait and the main job of the Pocono Summit Fire Department, when it finally responded, was to prevent fires from spreading.

Lugging an empty bucket in either hand, Faith ran down the road, trailing Ben and her mother. She ran until she felt her lungs would burst and then ran some more. Her mind was whirling, too, her sense of urgency forcing away every thought, until she finally burst into the little clearing that comprised the totality of Elvin Red-Moon's farm.

Red-Moon's house wasn't on fire—at least Faith was spared that—but his barn was engulfed in flames. Seven or eight people were already there and a bucket brigade had formed, running from the well to the barn, with Red-Moon tossing bucket after bucket of water onto the fire. Faith was quickly put to work, her job to pump the handle nonstop, and she worked until her arms ached and her body was pouring sweat. But she could see that the task was hopeless.

Putting out the raging flames with buckets of water was like trying to cool a volcano by spitting into the lava. Still, she was unprepared when the roof collapsed, sending up a column of fiery embers, or when the walls fell inward a moment later.

Now the battle was only to keep the fire from spreading to the house. Without anyone giving orders, the bucket line reformed, running from the well to the house, where Red-Moon had climbed a ladder to the roof. The buckets were passed to Ben Hightower, halfway up the ladder, who passed them on to Red-Moon, who calmly doused the smoldering embers.

"Give me a turn, Faith." The voice belonged to Paul Crow, who'd arrived, breathless, only a moment before. "Step away."

Faith tried to make sense of the words. All she knew was that she had to keep pumping. Yes, the situation was hopeless, and, yes, she was filling buckets faster than they could be emptied and the water was splattering on the ground beside the well. None of that mattered. She had to keep going.

Paul took Faith's arms and tugged her away. She fought him at first, yanking herself free of his grasp, but he persisted and she finally dropped to the ground. Without warning, her eyes filled with tears and her shoulders began to shake. At no time did Faith ask herself if the fire was an accident. She simply assumed, without actually deciding to, that Abe Hoskins was making good on his promise.

Of course, once the fire was out, the People held a council. Watching the meeting unfold, Faith found herself angry. Nothing had changed. Was the fire accidental? Those inclined to sell their property argued that it was, or at least there was no proof to the contrary. Those who were determined to stay argued that Red-Moon's barn wasn't a barn at all, but a workshop where he made the dugout canoes he sold to lakeside resorts. There was nothing inside—no gasoline or kerosene—to ignite. Furthermore, Red-Moon wasn't in the barn when the fire started. He was in the house, making breakfast.

Even Paul looked disgusted. He was off by himself, sitting on the stump of a tree, lost in thought. Faith was seated next to her mother, on a chair hauled from Red-Moon's kitchen. Margaret was sitting with her chin in her hands, apparently as disgusted as Paul Crow.

"It's stupid, right?" Faith asked.

"What?"

"All this talk. Because they'll never come to an agreement."

"Don't be too sure of that." Margaret gestured to Red-Moon. "Do you know what Red-Moon lost in the fire?"

"A canoe?"

"What else?"

"I don't know."

"Red-Moon makes a dugout canoe every winter, using the old methods."

"Like the canoe Paul and I use?"

"Exactly. The only difference is that Red-Moon paints the outside of his canoe with designs he picked up from a Navajo. The big resorts, the ones with lakes, display the canoes as authentic Indian memorabilia. Indians are very big in the region. Down in Milford they have the Hiawatha Stagecoach to carry tourists from the railroad to their hotels. The horses wear feathers on their heads."

Margaret stopped abruptly, her eyes fixed on Red-Moon. For a moment, Faith thought her mother was through speaking, but then Margaret went on.

"Red-Moon uses the money he makes on the canoes to pay his taxes in the fall. He's in serious trouble now that he's lost his canoe in the fire. You can gather food in the forest. You can feed yourself by hunting and fishing. But there's no money growing on those trees and the county assessors only accept cash."

Faith watched Red-Moon get to his feet. He didn't appear beaten or worried, or even angry about the loss of his canoe. He stood quietly for a moment, his gaze running over the others, before he began.

"I been thinkin'," he said, "about this offer we got from Scranton Properties. I been thinkin' somethin's wrong with how we're takin' it. You know how it is when somethin's ticklin' at the back of your mind, but you can't quite put your finger on it? Like an itch you can't quite reach? Well, somethin' come to me, somethin' I shoulda seen before, as I watched my barn burn this mornin'. See, there's one thing everybody agrees on. This offer we got is generous, much more than we could hope to get on the open market. Now, why would anybody pay that much for woodland that ain't no different from any other woodland 'round here? That's the question we been askin' ourselves, over and over. In fact, we become so stuck on that question, we completely missed another question. Yes, Scranton Properties has made a high offer—real high—but does that mean it's as high as they'll go?"

A tiny smile pulled at the edge of Red-Moon's mouth. Faith echoed that smile with a larger one of her own. He had them now. There wasn't a single member of the council doing anything but staring at Red-Moon, even Caleb Littlewolf, who'd been opposing Red-Moon throughout the endless discussion. Littlewolf was staring angrily at Red-Moon, as if he already knew he'd been out-maneuvered.

"Seems to me, if a company wants a particular property so bad it's willin' to pay three times what the acreage is worth, that same company might pay four times, or even five. The question is how to find out." Again Red-Moon paused, looking around. "One thing is sure, my brothers and sisters, negotiatin' one at a time is a losin' proposition. One family sells, then a second, then a third, then a fourth, until there's only a few left. That's when the company sweetens its offer. Course, that can't happen if we come to the table together, if we negotiate as a tribe, as the People. And one other thing you might want to consider. We can nose around while we negotiate, maybe even find out why Scranton Properties wants our land and how much it's really worth."

Red-Moon had been right. The offers were so good that not one of the families in favor of selling had considered the possibility that they were selling cheap. Now they came together, all except for Littlewolf, who tried to argue that the offers might be withdrawn if the company was pressured. But his objection was rapidly dismissed and Faith, as she watched, finally realized that for all the talk, all the disagreement, the People were profoundly bonded. These were folks who routinely aided each other, there being no thought of neglecting the sick or the old. Every man for himself, an idea so common in New York, didn't apply to their sense of community. They'd come together and they were glad of it. That was why they'd remained in council so long, enduring the same arguments over and over again. All in the hope of unity.

Well, Faith thought, *there's no other way. Not if Aunt Eva was telling the truth when she said that no Indian, no matter how powerful, had the right to tell another Indian what to do.*

Yet, at the same time, they were more closely bonded than the citizens of any modern country. Somehow, if they were to survive, they had to find consensus.

Unfortunately, the council was far from over. If consensus had been found on the general principle—they ought to negotiate as a unit—agreement on the details was a long way off. A committee had to be chosen and objectives defined. The discussion of one question alone, how much power the committee would have, threatened to outlast the Great Depression.

Finally, Margaret and another woman, Bernice Faircloud, volunteered to go back to Aunt Eva's and prepare a meal. Paul Crow and Faith went with them to fish. Everyone knew there wouldn't be much. Beans and greens and the last of the squash, whatever eggs could be found, and a package of ground venison from Bernice Faircloud's freezer. A few fish, freshly caught, would surely help.

By the time she and Paul reached the edge of the lake, Faith was almost running. She picked up the canoe's bow and pushed it into the water, leaping on board at the last minute. The canoe rocked as she settled her weight on the front crossbeam, then again when Paul hopped aboard. Prepared now, Faith shifted her weight effortlessly, righting the canoe. Then they were off, gliding onto the waters of Wildwood Lake, paddles dipping, Faith's tension instantly relieved. The past two days had been awful, among the worst she'd ever known. She needed to get away and the lake was just the place to accomplish that end.

In the distance, a V-shaped wake spread from a brown triangle in the water. The brown triangle was the head of a swimming beaver, the only part of the animal above water. You could tell beavers from otters because the beavers weren't playful; they always swam in a straight line. This particular beaver was headed for the southern end of the lake a quarter-mile away. There it would gnaw through the aspens and birch clustered near the shore then drag the small trees back to its lodge.

Closer to the canoe, a black wedge popped out of the water. This was the beak of a turtle that had come up from the bottom to breathe—the head of a snapping turtle judging from the size. Only a few yards away, a pair of Canadian geese herded their six goslings away, honking softly. The geese were eternally vigilant. Faith had seen them feeding on the lake's margin. The adults never ate together. While one plucked at the spring grasses, the other stood with its long neck extended upward, its head in constant motion.

With only a minimum of disgust, Faith baited her hook. She was facing forward, with her back to Paul Crow. Paul was silent, as usual, but Faith wasn't offended. She no longer believed that his silence was a show of contempt for her city ways. Paul was incapable of pretense. He wasn't acting a part. He was just who he was. And she was glad for it.

It was funny how Paul was so unlike any boy she'd ever known. Sure, he was still just a kid—and a stubborn one, at that—but he seemed to already have a strong idea about what his path in life would be. Stronger, certainly, than hers.

For a moment, Faith allowed herself to imagine what he'd be like in a few years, when he wouldn't be just a kid anymore, but a man. She actually had to stifle a laugh when she thought of what kind of husband he'd make.

"What?" Paul asked, overhearing her.

"Nothing." It was Faith's turn to be the silent type.

She cast her line ten feet out, let the baited hook drop to the bottom, and settled on the crossbeam that served as her seat. The sun had dropped just below the tops of the trees on the western side of the lake. Bolts of light streamed between the leaves to flash on the waters, while the spring leaves, lit from behind, might have been plucked from the stained glass windows of a cathedral.

"Can you get away tomorrow?" Paul asked. "There's something I want to show you."

Startled by Paul's voice, Faith took a moment to reply. She had no idea what Aunt Eva might be expecting of her on the following day, or what restrictions might be put on her activities. "Maybe in the afternoon," she finally said. "We've got to finish the pots before the clay dries. We're already behind. But what is it you want me to see?"

Paul Crow had done enough speaking. He limited his reply to, "I'd rather show you." Then he gave his line a tiny tug, just enough to make the bait tremble. An instant later, a hungry pickerel snatched the hook.

Fourteen

WHEN PAUL CROW and Faith Covington returned home with a string of bass, pickerel, and perch, they learned that the council had eventually reached an agreement. A committee of two had been appointed to meet with Scranton Properties. This committee wasn't authorized to actually negotiate, but only to explore the possibility of negotiation. That was great, according to Aunt Eva. The agreement was proof that councils actually worked. Unfortunately, the two men appointed to conduct the negotiations—Elvin Red-Moon and Caleb Littlewolf—were unlikely to agree on anything.

The main benefit was time, Aunt Eva told Faith as they stood before the kitchen sink. Margaret, after preparing a massive dinner, had been excused from further duties.

"I've got no intention of movin'," Aunt Eva explained, "but I'm hopin' these other fools will decide to stay if they have a little time to consider what they're givin' up. When Red-Moon's grandpa moved to the lake from North Dakota, him and his Sioux wife, there wasn't nobody livin' in these parts. The nearest town of any size was Milford, down in the valley. That's twenty miles away. Little by little, Samuel Red-Moon found others like himself, folks who traced their ancestors to some Lenape line, and convinced them to return to the land of their forebears. Now, this ain't no paradise we built around the lake. What we do is about workin' hard every day. But I tell you, honey, there's no other life I'd trade it for."

This wasn't the first time Faith had heard this speech, but she listened politely. Aunt Eva was looking her age for once. Maybe that was because the fire in Red-Moon's barn had raised an obvious, if unasked, question: What next?

"Aunt Eva?"

"Yes, honey?"

"Jaspin Gore spoke to you at church. You remember? When he came out after the service?"

"Sure."

"Well, I was wondering how you knew him."

"A long time ago, when he a little boy, I took care of Jaspin." Aunt Eva scrubbed a dish she'd already washed. She inspected the dish briefly then handed it over to Faith and smiled. "Girl, you just called up a lot of memories. When I first came here with my husband, Jonas, I wasn't but nineteen years old. Jonas, he set to building a house, but we still needed money for taxes and food 'til we could get a garden started. So I went to work for the Gore family, takin' care of their boy, Jaspin. He was two years old and their first child."

Faith dried the dish and set it atop a stack of dishes on the table. "If you know him that well, why was he so unfriendly to you? I mean, he did say hello, but he sure didn't seem happy to see you."

"Jaspin was the loneliest boy…" Aunt Eva paused for a moment as the memories flooded back. "The rich families

FINDING FAITH

on the other side of the woods, they don't raise their children the way we do. Here, the kids have chores and such, but parents don't watch 'em from dusk 'til dawn. We mostly let the children watch each other. There's a price to pay, of course, because accidents happen, especially in the woods and around the lake. Maybe that's why the white families keep their children close. Jaspin was barely allowed to leave the house, even with me to watch out for him, and he was never allowed in the woods. That boy, he didn't lay eyes on another child from one month to the next."

Faith thought of Pauline as Aunt Eva continued talking.

"I think that's why he grew up to be such a hard man. The way I heard, Jaspin doesn't treat his miners who work for him much better than slaves."

True to his word, Paul Crow arrived the next day shortly after noon. He carried his rifle with him, holding it against his chest with the barrel upward as if in some sort of strange salute. Faith and Aunt Eva were decorating the finished pots, inscribing the soft clay with a pattern of lines and symbols. The pots would be left to dry before they were fired because any moisture left in the clay would expand when the pots were heated, in which case they would burst. Two days of hard work with nothing to show for the effort was definitely not the Indian way. Better safe than sorry.

Aunt Eva and Faith lugged the pots to a corner of the barn and left them upright, then walked to the house through a soft, warm rain. Paul joined them there, as did Ben Hightower, who had passed the night hunting raccoons in the forest. Unlike those of Aunt Eva and Faith, Ben's efforts had not been rewarded.

"Raccoons are too smart," he complained at the table. "You can't hunt 'em without dogs."

"Ben, we've talked about this a hundred times." Aunt Eva shook her head. "I won't chain a dog any more than I'd chain a human being. You chain a dog, you chain its spirit."

Faith was the first to respond. "In Sunday school, they told us that animals don't have souls."

Margaret lightly kicked her daughter under the table. The message, as Faith understood it, was, "Watch your smart mouth." The conflicts between the Lenape religion and Christianity were not a subject to be discussed with Aunt Eva.

"I was talkin' about spirits, not souls," Aunt Eva said. "But you got the basic part right. *Kishelemukong*, who created the heavens and the earth, didn't give humans any priority. The least thing, even the worm you put on your hook, was important to him. Christianity places humans at the center of creation. In fact, you'd think from hearin' some Christians talk that humans are all God really cares about. I don't believe that's so."

"Then why do you go to church?" Faith asked the question without looking at her mother. She wasn't trying to goad Aunt Eva. She just wanted to know the answer. The teaching of the Presbyterian Church, one of which she and her parents attended back in Manhattan, was always presented as a revealed truth that couldn't be altered.

"Honey," Aunt Eva said, "maybe the best thing I can say about the religion of the old days was that we didn't have priests to tell us what was true and what wasn't. Religion was somethin' you went and found for yourself."

"So, there weren't any services?"

"I wouldn't say that. The People definitely had ceremonies. But we had no list of beliefs everyone had to swear to." Aunt Eva picked at her lunch. The meal was simple, to say the least—biscuits and blackberry preserves and coffee. "Funny thing about the settlers. They brought their missionaries with 'em, Moravian missionaries. The settlers aimed to save our souls while they robbed us blind. Mostly, the People didn't trust the missionaries, but some converted because they were fool enough to believe the missionaries would let 'em return to their land. Didn't happen, though."

Faith accepted Aunt Eva's answer, though she still didn't know why Aunt Eva, if she believed as she did, went to church on Sunday, or even why she thought of herself as a Christian. But Faith liked the idea of being free to choose. Because it seemed to her that if adults were smart enough to know the real truth about God, they would have been smart enough to prevent the Great Depression.

"Mom, do you think Paul and I could take a walk this afternoon? It's not raining very hard."

"Maybe," Paul chimed in, "we'll even come across one of those raccoons Ben was lookin' for last night."

The conversation stopped for just a second. Paul Crow had made a joke, and at Ben's expense—a rare moment.

"Next time, I'll take you with me," Ben said. "You can howl like a dog, scare them 'coons up a tree." When Paul didn't reply, Ben said, "What I think I'll do is set up some snares. I came across a trail 'round dawn that looks well used."

"Whereabouts?" Paul asked.

"To the south. But you keep away from there. I don't want you leavin' your scent on the trail."

Margaret raised a hand to stop the conversation. She had something to say and she made eye contact with Aunt Eva before she began to speak.

"Don't worry about the raccoons. Ben doesn't know it yet, but he's taking me into Mount Pocono this afternoon. I've got a little money and I plan to invest part of it in a beef stew with carrots and onions and potatoes, and a cake made with flour and sugar and milk and eggs." Margaret paused before adding, "And I plan to cover the cake with chocolate frosting."

Ben was first to react. He folded his hands, as if in prayer, and brought them to his chest. Then he raised his eyes to the ceiling and said, "Hallelujah, I'm saved at last."

Fifteen

AS BEFORE, WHEN Faith Covington entered the forest that afternoon, she sensed that she was leaving her old life behind, as if the thirteen years of her life were no longer relevant. She wore a borrowed canvas jacket and a peaked engineer's cap, also borrowed. The jacket had been treated with wax to keep out the rain, as had her boots, but neither protected her legs from the wet brush.

Paul Crow had even less protection from the damp weather, but he seemed not to notice. He kept up a steady pace, leading Faith along the banks of a familiar stream. The babble of the flowing waters over the rocks merged with the steady drip of water from a million leaves and branches to become one voice. There was no wind and the light rain fell through a heavy mist that blended with the pale shadows cast by the trees to create a world so vague and indistinct it seemed almost an illusion. Faith walked with her head down, her eyes on Paul's heels as she followed along.

They walked for thirty minutes, their only companions the songbirds moving in the branches overhead—cardinals, jays and sparrows, thrushes and finches. The birds, even the red cardinals, seemed without color, as if the world had thrown off its finery for the day and taken up the cloak of mourning. Faith didn't fight the mood. Instead, she kept her thoughts to herself, choosing to endure the discomfort without complaint, until Paul finally came to an abrupt halt and gestured to the right.

Faith stared out across a clearing in the dense woods created by a fallen oak, one of the forest giants. There were still leaves on the oak's branches, so recently had it dropped to the ground. Nevertheless, weeds and grasses had already taken advantage of the sunlight to spring up around the trunk and between the branches. On the other side of the clearing, a deer—a doe—stood with her head raised, a clump of grass still in her jaw. Beside the doe, almost lost in the mist, a tiny fawn tottered on unsteady legs. The fawn wanted to nurse but the doe was too nervous. She took a step, then another, head high, on full alert. Then she led her fawn into the deep woods, her steps so quiet they were lost in the splattering of raindrops on the leaves carpeting the forest floor.

"We need to be quiet from here on," Paul said.

"We haven't exactly been chatting up a storm until now. If we're going to be any quieter, we'll have to stop breathing."

Paul shook his head in disgust and continued on, following a path through heavy brush. He moved slowly, pausing to listen from time to time, until Faith finally admitted to herself that whatever danger Paul feared was far from imagined. Somehow, Faith found herself angry. If there was anything dangerous about what they were doing, she should have been informed before their walk began. Faith looked back the way they'd come. Could she find her way home by herself? Maybe, maybe not.

Faith was about to tap Paul on the shoulder and demand that he turn back, when he stopped abruptly. They were inside a tiny clearing, surrounded by young sugar maples, their branches sweeping almost to the earth.

"Wait here, Faith," Paul said. "Let me take a look around."

Paul was gone before Faith could frame an indignant response, which only served to fuel her indignation. Leave her alone? In the middle of nowhere? When she finally returned to the farm, she'd have a word with Paul Crow. In fact, she might punctuate her remarks by smacking the boy right on the head. Whatever he was up to didn't involve her. She wasn't one of the People. They had her sympathies, for what happened to them in the past and what was happening in the present, but their problems were not hers.

Faith slowly calmed as the minutes passed. Her cap was soaked through, her hair as well, and her sopping coveralls were plastered to her legs. But the day was warm and she wasn't uncomfortable.

Gradually, her attention turned to the rain as it fell on the wide leaves of the maples, as the drops formed little pools that became rivulets, cascading from leaf to leaf until they disappeared into the moss on the forest floor. Off in the distance, so faint she thought at first that she was imagining it, an owl called—*hoo, hoo, hooooooo*—its mournful cry blending with the shadows and the mist and the steady patter of rain in the leaves. Faith felt, for just a moment, as if the forest itself were calling out—and calling out to her—though in a language she couldn't fathom. Then Paul Crow slipped into the clearing.

"It's okay," he said, "there's no one around."

The owl cried again and Faith shuddered. "Paul Crow, if you leave me alone again, I swear I'll knock you down."

Faith was half-kidding, but Paul took her seriously, as he seemed to take everything seriously. "I had to make sure there was no one guarding the mine," he said. "I couldn't take you with me because you make too much noise when you walk."

After a moment's consideration, Faith decided to let the last part, the insult, pass. "What mine are you talking about?"

"The mine I brought you out here to see." Paul turned and slid between the branches of the maples. "It's not far."

Not far turned out to be a ten-minute walk over slippery ground to a low hill. On the slope of the hill, Faith saw what she initially took for a cave. That was because the entrance wasn't squared off the way she imagined a mine to be. But as they came closer and she was able to see into the darkness, she noticed rounded columns, almost like tree trunks, lining both sides of the narrow shaft, and squared timbers overhead. Curiously, there were no buildings anywhere, and no road. They were in dense forest.

"What's going on?" she asked. "Why isn't there anyone around?"

"The mine was abandoned a long time ago." Paul continued to scan his surroundings. He was carrying his shotgun, holding the weapon across his chest. "We're only a few hundred yards from where Crease Marron fired on you and Aunt Eva. That's what got me suspicious."

"You don't think Crease shooting at us was an accident?"

"No. You were being warned to keep away. But keep away from what? There's a road, but it's about a half mile from here and there's nothing on either side except more forest. Then I remembered the old mine and I decided to explore a bit. Look, try to stay on the leaves when you walk.

If you step in the mud, you'll make footprints and I don't want anyone to know we've been here."

As they approached the mine, Faith saw footprints, dozens of them, created by the boots of an adult. She also noticed, very faintly, the outlines of a home's foundation and a long cascade of rocks where a chimney had collapsed.

"I don't get this at all. What kind of mine is this?"

"Coal."

"Then why is it abandoned?"

"Most likely because there wasn't enough coal." Paul shook the rain out of his hair. "From what Red-Moon told me, there was a lot of exploration up here about seventy-five years ago, but none of it panned out. The big coal mines are in the valley to the west. That's why the railroad was built."

"The Lackawanna Railroad?"

"Right. They built it after the Civil War to haul coal to New York." Paul smiled, the smile seeming to Faith apologetic. "According to Red-Moon, at least."

Closer now, Faith heard the owl call: *Hoo, hoo, hooooooo.*

"Is Red-Moon some kind of historian?" Faith asked.

"He's a historian of the People. Red-Moon says that the history in books is all about the white man. He says the Indians have been left out."

Faith was going to say, "Well, if it's all about the white *man*, then women have been left out, too." But she was getting better at learning to keep her mouth shut at the right times.

"What's coal mining have to do with the People?" she asked instead.

Stumped, Paul shook his head. "There's something else I want you to see," he said. "Closer to the road."

Faith followed Paul through the forest for several hundred yards. She noticed broken tree branches on the ground, and more footprints in the muddier spots. But Paul didn't pause until he found the particular object he was looking for, a narrow post with white-and-red markings on one end.

"That's a surveyor's pole," he said.

"How long has it been here?"

"The paint's still bright and it's lying on top of the leaves, so it can't be very long. The road I told you about is just beyond those beech trees."

Faith started to reply then held up, content to watch a red squirrel scamper through the branches of an ancient hemlock while she gathered her thoughts. The animal moved with an unconscious grace that she, a mere human being, could never hope to match.

"The coal mine thing explains why Scranton Properties wants to pay so much for the land," she finally said. "At least if you assume they're connected. Do you know whose land we're on?"

"That's why I didn't tell you about the mine right away. I wanted to check my father's survey map first."

"And?"

"The land we're on right now belongs to the state of Pennsylvania. The state controls the land on both sides of the road for a quarter of a mile. But the coal mine? That's on Caleb Littlewolf's land."

"Caleb Littlewolf, who keeps telling everyone to sell?"

"None other."

Paul led the way back toward the community, while Faith tracked the route, mapping the various twists and turns in her mind. There was no reason to linger; the possibility that somebody was assigned to patrol the area could hardly be ignored. Wasn't that exactly what Crease Marron was doing when he happened on Faith and Aunt Eva? Now they were going to lay the whole thing out for... Well, that was the crux of a dispute they ironed out once they were clear of the mine. Faith wanted to go first to Aunt Eva then to Red-Moon. Paul, of course, wished to inform his mentor immediately.

"Why, because Red-Moon's a man?" Faith asked.

"He'll know what to do next."

"Of course he'll know what to do next. Even I know what to do next. Even the turtles in the lake know what to do next. Call a council meeting."

They were still discussing the matter when the unmistakable crack of a rifle produced an instant, frozen silence. Red-Moon's home lay around a sharp bend in the road not a hundred yards away. Faith's first instinct was to dash into the woods, an instinct reinforced by the sound of a car starting. What if the car headed toward them? Then it would be too late... But Paul was off and running, running toward Red-Moon's little farm, and Faith wasn't about to desert him. Reluctantly, she followed him around the bend only to discover an empty road before them.

The bitter stench of charred wood from the barn, now soaked with rain, rose up to greet Paul and Faith as they stepped onto Red-Moon's property. This close to the lake and driven by a light breeze, the fog swirled and danced, obscuring the house only fifty feet away. Lying motionless in the tall, wet grass, Red-Moon went unseen until Faith came within a few yards of his body. Then she raised a trembling finger.

"Paul...?"

"Yes?"

"There, over there."

Paul didn't panic. He took a few steps forward and knelt down beside Red-Moon. He shook the older man's shoulder. "Red-Moon? Red-Moon!"

The old man didn't respond, not to the first shake, nor the second, nor the third. Paul's eyes rose to meet Faith's and it was all she could do not to cry out at the look of despair on his face. Suddenly, she found the courage to approach Red-Moon, to kneel beside Paul, to ignore the blood covering the side of Red-Moon's head, to lay her ear against his chest. Faith was sure she'd find nothing, already imagining him dead and cold, but Red-Moon's heart was beating. Very slowly, true, and when she placed her fingers on his wrist, she was unable to detect a pulse, but he was definitely alive.

"His heart's beating, Paul," she said. "I'm going to Aunt Eva's. You get a blanket from the house, try to keep him warm."

Faith didn't wait for a reply. She headed off down the muddy road, trying to stay on the margins where it was less slippery. She fell, nonetheless, three times, ripping both knees of her coveralls. Her wet hair came loose to whip against her face, and her jacket was smeared with mud when she finally burst into Aunt Eva's kitchen, so out of breath she could barely speak.

Margaret Covington raised a hand to her mouth. She reached out for her daughter, sure she was injured, but Faith waved her away.

"It's Red-Moon," she gasped. "Red-Moon's been shot."

Sixteen

ELVIN RED-MOON WAS still in the grass when the four of them—Faith Covington, Margaret, Ben, and Aunt Eva—arrived in Ben's truck. His head was lying on a pillow and Paul had covered him with a blanket. Except for the bloody wound on the right side of his head, he might have been asleep.

Aunt Eva was the first to speak. "If he was shot, the bullet didn't penetrate. There's no hole in his skull. Maybe he'll be all right. Let's get him in the house."

"He needs to go to a hospital right away," Margaret said. "He needs medical treatment."

"You're right, but takin' him in the bumpy bed of a pickup truck while it's rainin' won't do him no good a'tall. Besides, the hospital in Tannersville ran out of money two months ago and closed down. And the one in Stroudsburg—thirty miles away by road—is barely able to keep its doors open."

"So, you're not going to do anything?"

"Margaret, in my life I doctored up more folks than I can count. But I'm still gonna send for Doc Murchison. If he says Red-Moon needs a hospital, I'll figure out some way to get him there. Maybe it'll stop rainin' by then."

Faith stood off by herself, again reluctant to approach the fallen Red-Moon. She watched the four of them—Ben, Aunt Eva, Paul, and Margaret—haul Red-Moon into the house, remembering the man's gentle humor and persuasive ways. She tried to tell herself that his injury was the result of an accident, that no one deliberately hurt the older man, that the crack she'd heard wasn't a rifle shot, but the car backfiring. But it only took a moment to dispel that notion. There was nothing in the grass, no rock, for instance, to account for his injury, even if he'd tripped while walking or simply passed out. And the only blood was on the ground where he fell.

Ben and Paul came out of the house, jumped in Ben's pickup truck and tore down the road, the pickup's rear end skidding off to one side before Ben got it under control. Margaret stepped into the yard a moment later, headed for the well. She was carrying a basin, which she hastily filled. At the same time, a puff of smoke rose from the house chimney, the humidity in the air holding the smoke close against the roof so that it was only gradually borne sideways toward the lake.

"Will he live?" Faith asked her mother.

"I don't know, honey. Red-Moon's not responding." Margaret laid the basin down on the well and approached her daughter. She took Faith in her arms, squeezing her tight. "I never meant to expose you to any of this," she said. "From here on, I want you to stay close to me. I don't know what they'll do next."

"Who are *they*, Mom? And why can't they be stopped? Why doesn't somebody call the police?"

Faith's last question answered itself two hours later, an hour after Dr. Murchison arrived, when Constable Abe Hoskins, notified by the doctor, drove up in his Buick. Murchison had been all business up until then. He'd examined Red-Moon thoroughly before leveling with Aunt Eva. Red-Moon had a fractured skull, probably resulting from a bullet that struck him a glancing blow and deflected away. His pupils were dilated and uneven, the left being noticeably more expanded. Every indication was that his brain had been damaged by the initial attack, but the greater threat was from subsequent swelling, which was probably taking place even as they spoke. The pressure of a swollen brain against the skull could result in any number of neurological problems, including seizures, or even death.

"If he wakes up and asks for water, don't give him any," Dr. Murchison explained. "You need to keep his fluid levels down."

"What about surgery?" Margaret asked.

"The nearest hospital with a brain surgeon is in Scranton. The trip would be as likely to kill him as his injury. I've given him a sedative to make sure he stays quiet and I'll stop back to see him tomorrow. Remember, don't give him anything to drink. And if he does become agitated, you'll have to restrain him."

Dr. Murchison was about to leave when Abe Hoskins held up a restraining hand. "Doc? I got a question needs answerin' before you run off. I'm speakin' here in my law enforcement capacity."

"Now that's rich, Abe," Dr. Murchison snorted with obvious contempt. "Considering you don't have an office, or even a jail."

Constable Hoskins' neutral expression didn't change. "Don't matter. Unless the sheriff's around, I'm the law in

Albemarle Township." He winked. "And the sheriff ain't around."

"All right, Abe." Dr. Murchison laid his leather bag on the back seat of his Ford. "How can I help you?"

"Was Red-Moon attacked? Or did he have some kind of accident?"

Dr. Murchison laughed loud and long. When he finally calmed down, he climbed into the front seat of his car and rolled down the window. "Red-Moon was shot—whether deliberately or by accident, I can't say. Now what you need to do, Abe, is call in Sheriff Garber. This business is way beyond your expertise."

"That ain't likely to happen, Doc. A body floated up in the Delaware yesterday and Sheriff Garber's gotta deal with it before he can get up here."

"Are you telling me that you notified the sheriff's office?"

Abe Hoskins took a hunk of chewing tobacco from a pouch and shoved it into his mouth. His jaws worked for a moment, then he spat a stream of brown tobacco juice onto the grass. "Sure did," he said.

When they were questioned by Constable Hoskins, both Paul and Faith failed to mention Paul's discovery of the coal mine or that Caleb Littlewolf owned the land. That was due, in part, because Hoskins didn't ask them where they were coming from when they discovered Red-Moon's body. His focus was on Red-Moon's state.

"He didn't say anything?" Hoskins asked.

"Nothing," Paul said.

"You sure?"

Hoskins was standing with his hands on his hips, glaring at Paul Crow, but Paul was apparently unafraid. He kept his eyes riveted to the constable's. Paul's mother stood beside him, as Margaret Covington stood beside her daughter. Nearly everyone from the community had shown up by then.

"Red-Moon was unconscious when we arrived," Paul insisted.

"How 'bout you, little lady?" Hoskins turned to Faith. "Did you hear Red-Moon say anything? Did he say who might have attacked him?"

Margaret stepped in before Faith answered. "Don't you bully my daughter," she said. "I won't have it. Your question has already been answered."

"What about the car? You said you heard a car start up." Hoskins looked again at Faith. "Did you actually see a car?"

"If she had," Margaret said, "she would have already told you so. Now stop harassing my daughter."

Hoskins shook his head, but didn't pursue the matter. There were too many people around by then.

"I'm gonna have to take your boy's shotgun," he told Paul's mother. "You best tell him to give it up."

"What do you want it for?" Winona Crow asked. "Red-Moon was shot with a rifle."

"If that's how it happened, the kid's got nothin' to worry about."

Paul handed the gun to Hoskins before his mother could respond. "Careful," he said, "it's loaded."

It took Faith a moment to realize that Paul was making a joke—a joke at Abe Hoskins' expense. But if Hoskins noticed, his expression didn't change. He turned away, dismissing Paul and Faith. Faith watched him cross the yard, thinking, initially, that she and Paul had triumphed, or at least held their own. But then she realized that Hoskins had discovered the one fact he really needed to establish.

Red-Moon's attacker was as yet unidentified. Now Hoskins was free to act as he chose.

Faith's judgment was more or less confirmed when Crease Marron arrived in a rusted Dodge coupe that had to be ten years old. With Marron to back him up, Hoskins began to approach the men from the community, confronting them one at a time, demanding they account for their whereabouts that morning. As he went along, he punctuated his questions by spitting on the ground.

Not everyone complied. Ben Hightower just shook his head, and Aunt Eva—the only woman approached—got right to the point when asked for an alibi. "Go on back to whoever sent you here, Abe. Tell 'em I'll give my alibi right after I hear yours."

Faith expected Hoskins to react to the various challenges, but he remained calm. Crease Marron did, too. Then Paul tapped Faith's shoulder and she finally turned away.

"Faith?"

"Yes."

"Come out to the road. I want to show you something."

Reluctantly, Faith followed Paul to the spot where they'd rounded the bend in the road. "I hope you're not headed back to the mine, Paul," she said, "because I've had enough for one day."

"No, I just wanted to tell you that I saw the car we heard start up. Over there, see, between those two white pines? The road passes just on the other side."

"And you saw the car?"

"Just for a second. Actually, it was a pickup truck, not a car." He shrugged. "I think maybe I know whose truck it is."

"Why didn't you say something?"

"I want to be sure. Besides, who should I tell? Abe Hoskins? Crease Marron?"

"How about Aunt Eva or Ben? You don't think they're on your side?"

"It's not that. See, I want him to think he got away clean."

"He? Why don't you tell me who *he* is?"

"Not until I'm sure."

"Paul, you can't go out there. You just can't. There's a killer out there and if he finds you snooping around, he won't hesitate. You're twelve years old, for goodness sake. This isn't some game."

"Red-Moon was my guide, Faith. My mentor. My friend. I can't desert him now, him or his spirit."

A moment later, Paul Crow slipped into the woods.

Seventeen

THERE WAS NO community council for once. Instead, the People, including Winona Crow and her husband, dispersed after a time, leaving Red-Moon to Aunt Eva's care while Faith Covington and Margaret went home to cook. When Ben and Margaret had gone to town earlier in the day, Margaret intended to prepare a meal that all would remember. But there was no cause for celebration now. Faith sat at the table, peeling potatoes and carrots and onions. The onions, as she began to quarter them, brought forth tears that were lurking close to the surface in any event.

"If things...don't work out here, where would we go?" she asked her mother.

"We're not going anywhere, honey. Not unless your father finds a job. Then we're going home."

"But we don't have a home." Faith's voice rose, her emotions whipping back and forth between anger and despair. She'd been raised to believe that people had a right to what they earned, what they bought with honest money, what they scrimped and saved over the years to acquire. So, how could a bank simply close its doors, taking the life savings of thousands of families with it? How could somebody who just wanted to keep his land be shot down like a rabid dog? And where was the law she was taught to respect?

"Home is any place we're all together." Margaret dredged the cubes of stew beef in flour and dropped them into a hot skillet, one piece at a time. "Me and you and your father. The where of it doesn't matter that much."

"But if they didn't steal our money, we'd still have our house."

"Who are *they*?"

"The bank."

"The bank went out of business, Faith. The bank's owners lost everything, too. That can't happen anymore…"

"Why?"

"Because deposits are insured by the government now." Margaret began to flip the chunks of stew beef, her aim to sear all sides. When she spoke, her tone was softer. "Too late for us, though. We have to start all over again."

Faith busied herself with cutting the potatoes. She'd been helping her mother prepare meals for the past couple of years and the chore was routine. As she understood the matter, her work in the kitchen was preparing her to be a wife and mother, to follow a path mapped out long ago—a path to a successful life. That path seemed more like a dead-end now.

"I'm not going to do it," she said.

"Do what?"

"What everyone says I have to do. I mean, it's like I'm in school and following all the rules—I raise my hand before speaking; I do my homework; I respect my teachers—but I get punished anyway. Isn't that what happened to Daddy? He followed all the rules and we have nothing to show for it."

Margaret removed the seared beef from the skillet and laid the chunks on a plate. Then she added some water, which sizzled and popped in the pan, and then added wild garlic and several bay leaves before scraping the pan to release the bits stuck to the bottom. Finally, she smiled.

"Everything you say is true, honey. The big speculators on Wall Street who got us into this mess didn't follow any of the rules and the whole country's paying the price. But at least there's hope now. Like I said before, bank deposits are insured by the government, so no family should ever lose its life savings again. And if your father's hired, he'll be hired by one of President Roosevelt's New Deal agencies. The president's putting millions of people to work."

Faith watched her mother stir the pot. She wasn't going to argue. Maybe President Roosevelt would make good on his campaign promises, maybe he'd give ordinary people like the Covingtons a new deal. Faith didn't know enough about politics to have a real opinion. But the shocks—all of them, from the day the stock market crashed in 1929 until the crack of a rifle echoed through the forest—couldn't just be erased because the government decided to give the little people a break. Anything could be taken away, a lifetime of hard work obliterated in a moment. Forget the rules. Faith Covington would think for herself from now on. Just like Aunt Eva.

They let the stew cool (the promised cake would be saved for a better day), then lugged the heavy pot all the way to Red-Moon's.

To Faith's relief, Red-Moon was still alive. He was moving his arms and legs from time to time, though he had yet to open his eyes. Faith supposed that was good news, but she was nevertheless mindful of Dr. Murchison's blunt prognosis: Red-Moon's brain would swell during the night. How much was anyone's guess.

Aunt Eva's blessing over their meal that night was extended. She spoke directly to her Creator, recounting the many times Red-Moon had come to the aid of others, whether individuals in need, or the community as a whole.

"To the extent that he was able, Red-Moon has followed his conscience all his life, and he deserves better than to die at the hand of a coward," she said. "But if You should choose to take him, Lord, I hope You can find it in Your blessed heart to let him into Your kingdom. Because if a man like Red-Moon isn't good enough for heaven, then heaven must be a lonely place. Amen."

That said, they ate mostly in silence, consuming every last bit of the stew despite the somber mood. There was coffee after dinner, dark and bitter, but no dessert. They were just finishing their coffee when they heard a car drive up.

"This better not be Abe Hoskins," Ben said. "Nor his deputy, neither. I've had enough of them two scoundrels for one day."

Aunt Eva went to the door, and then stepped into the yard. Margaret followed her, along with Ben, but Faith chose to stay in the doorway. The car parked by the side of the road wasn't Abe Hoskins' Oldsmobile. The man leaning on the sleek black Cadillac was Jaspin Gore. He wore a suede jacket, shiny leather boots that rose above the cuffs of his trousers, and a western hat, a gray Stetson with a six-inch brim.

Behind Jaspin Gore, Pauline's little head was framed by the car's open window. Though the rain had stopped and the sky was rapidly clearing, the evening was cool enough to justify her violet coat and matching cloche, if not the expression on her face. The younger girl was staring at Faith's torn and muddy overalls, her eyes wide with disbelief. As for Faith, she raised a hand and waved, but didn't speak.

"What are you doin' here?" Ben asked.

Gore turned to Aunt Eva, his steel-gray eyes cold and hard. "Is that any way to treat a visitor? I've come to pay my respects. Red-Moon's been living in these parts longer than my own family."

"Your family never lived here," Ben said. "Your family lives in mansions in Scranton and New York. You only come up here to kill animals you don't eat."

Aunt Eva stepped in to break the tension. "Red-Moon ain't up to havin' visitors, Jaspin, if that's why you come."

"Sorry to hear that." Gore's eyes flicked to what remained of the barn. "Seems like somebody doesn't want him around."

"Or any of the rest of us." Aunt Eva crossed her arms. "Tell me, Jaspin, did Scranton Properties make an offer on your land?"

"Never heard of them. But I'm glad I found you here. The board of supervisors for Albemarle Township held an emergency meeting this afternoon."

"With you running the show?"

"I'm the president of the board, Eva, but I don't give the orders. I merely preside over meetings." Gore paused long enough to smile. "This particular meeting was about schools and roads. Now, I realize this is old news, but I'll repeat it anyway. Our schools are short-handed, the township's roads are falling apart and our tax revenues have fallen off. The board was hoping the state would make up the shortfall, but our request for funding was turned down. Thus, we had no choice except to share the burden equally by raising property taxes. I just thought, as long as I was here, I'd give you advance notice."

Aunt Eva's expression darkened as she put her hands on her hips. "How much, Jaspin? How much will it cost me?"

"Well, I can't say exactly. The assessments won't go out for a month or so."

"Jaspin, you were a bad liar when you were two years old and you're a bad liar now. How much?"

Though Gore's smile broadened, his eyes remained hard. "You're acting as though you've been singled out. The increase affects every homeowner in the township, including me."

"What about the resorts? The inns and the hotels?"

"Now, Eva, the resorts provide the only real jobs in the township. We can't very well tax them out of business."

"No, you can't, especially because a majority of the men on the board of supervisors are resort owners. If you had tried to increase their taxes, they'd have voted you down. But tell me how much, Jaspin. Is the increase enough to drive us out?"

"I'm not privy to your resources…"

"How much, Jaspin?"

Gore shook his head. "About fifty percent. Just enough to balance the budget. Which, of course, we have to do by law."

"And who wrote the budget?"

"The board, of course."

Disgusted, Faith turned her gaze from Jaspin Gore to his daughter, Pauline. A series of calculations followed closely behind. Aunt Eva depended on the tourist trade for the cash she needed to pay her taxes. The Depression had affected the tourist trade, with a dwindling number of families coming to the mountain every summer. Less money from her little stand. Higher taxes in the fall. Aunt Eva was in serious trouble, as were the other Lenape families.

Pauline chose that moment to speak out for the first time. "Hi, Faith," she called. "What are you doing this summer? Are you having fun?"

Faith found herself with nothing to say. Despite Pauline's lovely coat and her perfectly coiffed hair and her Cadillac and her many homes, what Faith felt for Pauline was closer to pity than it was to envy.

Except for a few wispy clouds, the skies had cleared by the time Margaret and Faith walked to the lake at ten o'clock that night. A nearly full moon, bright enough to overpower the surrounding stars, lent a silvery edge to the wake of a swimming beaver. Hundreds of bats swooped and dove, executing impossible turns in search of the insects they fed upon. At the far horizon, a shooting star flashed to earth, followed by a second and a third. The night was alive.

"Why did you bring me to the lake?" Margaret asked her daughter.

"Because I can think here."

A loon called from across the water, an otherworldly yodel that rose through several octaves before ending on a note so lonely that Faith shuddered. Then an owl—her owl—glided onto the lowest branch of a red maple standing at the water's edge. The bird's wings settled against its sides and it began to hoot. *Hoo, hoo, hooooooo.* In the moonlight, its overlapping feathers were the color of polished armor.

Faith took a step toward the owl, hoping the animal would fly away. She couldn't shake a hardening belief that the owl had come for her, that it carried a message. The bird didn't move a muscle at her approach.

"Mom?" Faith finally turned away. "There's something I have to tell you."

"What's that, honey?"

"It's about Paul. He thinks he knows who shot Red-Moon."

"How? You told us you were out of sight when the shot was fired."

"That's true, only Paul saw a pickup truck driving away and he thinks he knows who owns it. I never did see the truck, but I heard it. Mom, Paul wants to snoop around on his own. He doesn't trust the constable and I don't blame him. But I'm afraid he'll get in trouble."

Margaret took a moment to think it over then asked, "Did Paul name the man he suspects?"

"No. I asked, but he wouldn't tell me."

"Faith, why didn't you speak up before now? Paul could be in danger."

"I promised Paul I wouldn't."

"And you think that's a good reason?"

The owl hooted twice and Faith turned to discover that the bird was looking directly at her. Refusing to be drawn into those pale yellow eyes, she focused on the owl's hooked beak and razor-sharp talons. There was nothing soft and cuddly about the animal. She was looking at a predator, not the Easter bunny.

"When Paul finds out I told on him," she said, "he'll probably never speak to me again." *Not that he spoke much before*, she thought.

"Faith, you've done the right thing. Paul is only twelve."

"That's exactly what I said to him, but he's got a real hard head, Mom. He thinks he's a warrior."

Eighteen

FAITH COVINGTON AND Margaret went first to Paul Crow's home, hoping against hope to find him in his bed. No such luck. Judson and Winona Crow had arrived from their work at Jaspin Gore's only a few moments before to find the house empty. They'd assumed, wrongly, that Paul was at Red-Moon's.

"Tell them," Margaret demanded.

Faith drew a breath before complying. She was angry at herself, at Paul, at the whole mess she and her mother had walked into. Nevertheless, she kept her tone neutral as she repeated the facts. Paul had seen a pickup truck fleeing the scene just after Red-Moon was shot. He thought he recognized the truck, but wasn't positive and wanted to investigate on his own. She hadn't known this when she first spoke to her mother and Aunt Eva. Paul told her later—hours later—when they were standing on the road and there was no one around to stop him from going off by himself. Still, she should have told her mother right away and she hadn't.

Done, Faith folded her arms across her chest. She hadn't mentioned one obvious fact. Even if she'd run back to Red-Moon's and told her mother everything, Paul was already gone. The community could have mounted a dozen search parties. They could have shouted his name until their throats were on fire and their voices gave out. Paul Crow wouldn't be found unless he wanted to be found.

They left for Red-Moon's within minutes, driving the short distance in the Crows' Dodge coupe. Winona Crow was sure they'd discover Paul at Red-Moon's, sure that her son would never leave Red-Moon's side while his life was in danger. But although Red-Moon was still unconscious, Paul was nowhere to be found.

Aunt Eva was by Red-Moon's side in the little home's single bedroom when they arrived. Ben Hightower sat in Red-Moon's kitchen, downing one cup of coffee after another. There'd been a new development in the hours since Faith and Margaret left—a clue uncovered by Ben when he visited Red-Moon's outhouse, lantern in hand.

"I was over by the woodshed where Red-Moon keeps his tools, and I noticed a can of oil that had a bullet hole right through the middle. Now I know Red-Moon ain't the kinda man to shoot targets in his yard, nor the kinda man to leave his garbage around, so I took me a closer look and found oil soaked into the ground, fresh oil. That got me suspicious and I dug in the grass 'til I come up with this here bullet."

The bullet in question was on the kitchen table. Though slightly bent, it was in good enough condition to stand on its end.

"I hear the police have a way now to tell what gun fired a particular bullet," Ben said. "I read about it in *True*

Detective, the magazine. Thing is, though, I can't see handin' the bullet over to Abe Hoskins. Most likely, it'd just up and disappear."

Paul's actual disappearance presented the same problem. How could they notify Constable Hoskins without telling him about Paul's sighting of the pickup truck or Ben's recovery of the bullet? Hoskins wasn't acting in their interests; he couldn't be trusted. Informing him would only place Paul in greater jeopardy, assuming he was in jeopardy at all. With the possible exception of Red-Moon, no Indian knew the forest better than Paul, who'd been drawn to it from his earliest years. And this wasn't the first time he'd spent a night in the woods. Far from it. Only last autumn, during hunting season, Paul was gone four days before returning with a ten-point buck that probably weighed more than he did.

"Who's to say Paul won't come home tonight?" Aunt Eva asked. "Or that he isn't there right now? Besides, since we don't know who he suspects, we don't know where to start lookin'. It's a big forest out there."

"Eva," Winona said, "Paul's my only child."

Aunt Eva put her arm around the younger woman. "I know, Winona, and if he's not home by tomorrow morning, we'll organize a search party at first light." She sighed and shook her head. "We've been tryin' to get telephones in here for ten years. They got 'em on the other side, on the white people's side, but every time we ask, the telephone company tells us they're lookin' into it. Lookin' into it? Lands, you'd think our money would be as good as anyone else's, but somehow it never happens."

Faith spoke up, surprising everyone. "If you organize a search party, you'll have to tell everybody why Paul went into the woods. How do you know you won't be telling the very man Paul suspects? How do you know that you won't be telling the man who tried to kill Red-Moon?"

"We'll only use folks in the community," Aunt Eva countered.

"Those are the ones I'm worried about, Aunt Eva. Paul told me he saw a pickup truck, one he thought he recognized. Well, if Paul recognized the truck, it must belong to someone who lives in the community. Constable Hoskins doesn't drive a truck."

Ben was the first to respond. "I don't take easy to the notion we have a traitor among the People," he said. "But it wouldn't be the first time we been sold out by one of our own. The girl's makin' sense, Eva. Come morning, if Paul ain't back, me and Judson will go look for him. Just the two of us."

Judson Crow lifted his head at the mention of his name. Tall and powerfully built, he could have been a warrior, but had chosen his path after long and careful deliberation. Now his plans were falling apart. His son was missing and the tax increase enacted by the township board threatened the entire community.

"There's somethin' I need to get off my chest," he announced. "That man from Scranton Properties who came around makin' offers on our homes? That would be Mr. Stanley Clark. He's been to visit Jaspin Gore, and more than once. Abe Hoskins has been around, too…and Crease Marron."

Aunt Eva shook her head. "When I asked Jaspin if Scranton Properties made him an offer, he claimed that he never heard of them. Guess I shouldn't be surprised. Did you hear what they said?"

Winona Crow spoke up. "No, they went into Mr. Gore's study and spoke privately. Look, I know we should have said something before now, but it's just… Well, I feel like employers have a right to privacy. But these people have gone too far." She hesitated, looking down at the tabletop. "I want to get home, Judson," she said. "I've never felt so helpless in all my life."

Judson Crow took his wife's arm and led her to the door. He paused there for a moment, his features composed. Then he said, "If anything's happened to my son, I mean to have justice. Jaspin Gore thinks he's big enough to get away with anything. He thinks he can't be touched. He'll find out different, though. As God is my witness."

Faith barely slept that night. And it wasn't the owl with its incessant hooting that kept her awake. Faith was torn by guilt. She should never have let Paul go off by himself. She had no way to stop him, of course. Paul made his own decisions, at least when his parents were at work. But she couldn't shake off the feeling that she should have gone with him. Sneaking off into the woods? Deserting her mother? Faith knew the very idea was crazy. Even if Paul had agreed, which was highly unlikely, she would only have gotten in his way.

But, still... Maybe it would have been better to be with him.

Faith closed her eyes and let her head drop to the pillow. The air was filled with the peeping of the frogs. Aunt Eva had called them tree frogs but that wasn't right, at least according to Paul. The spring peepers did climb trees, he explained, but they lived mostly in swampy areas around the lake, foraging for insects on the ground. Well, that was the thing about Paul. He knew more about the forest, and how to travel through it, than any adult in the community except Red-Moon. He could take care of himself.

Exhausted, Faith longed for sleep. She'd always been a good sleeper, even as a young child, usually drifting off within a few minutes. Now her brain was twisting and turning like the bats she'd watched earlier in the evening, as if her mind was seeking an answer to a question that hadn't been asked.

Outside, a cool breeze whistled through the leaves at the forest's edge, a moan echoed in the calls of a loon. Faith lay with the blankets pulled up to her throat, imagining Paul in the woods, half-frozen. But that wasn't right. Paul would find a sheltered spot and make a fire, as he'd done so many times before.

The full moon had dropped in the west to stand just above the treetops. Its pale light, streaming through the window, splashed across Faith's bed. She felt her gaze drawn to the silvery disc, as if she were looking into the eye of a living creature. The owl continued to call, again and again—*hoo, hoo, hooooooo*—in a voice so familiar that Faith felt the need to frame an answer. But there was no question asked, at least none she could put her finger on, and she finally dropped into a fitful sleep.

Faith and Margaret had breakfast shortly after dawn. Faith fed the chickens while her mother fried eggs fresh from the nests. Neither bothered with the dishes and they were off to Red-Moon's before the sun cleared the trees on the eastern edge of the yard, only to discover that nothing had changed. Red-Moon stirred from time to time, but he was still unconscious. Winona and Judson Crow had stopped by. Paul hadn't returned, either to his own home or to Red-Moon's. Nevertheless, there was one surprise and it came from Margaret, not Aunt Eva or Ben or the Crows.

"I want you to drive me to the train station in Pocono Summit, Ben," she announced. "I'm going to the sheriff's office in Stroudsburg. We've got one man wounded and a child missing. This can't go on."

A discussion followed, naturally, much to Faith's disgust. Sheriff Lee Garber, Aunt Eva insisted, was no friend of the Indian community. He'd be as likely to go to Jaspin Gore as come to their aid. Ben echoed Aunt Eva's assessment, but Margaret was adamant.

"If the sheriff won't listen, I'll go to the state police. What's going on here has to stop, Aunt Eva. It has to."

"How will you get back, Mom?" Faith asked. "There are no telephones."

"We'll check the schedule when we get to the station and arrange a pickup time. But, look, honey, I want you to stay at Aunt Eva's while I'm—"

"You're not taking me?"

"No, it's better if I do this myself. I mean to confront the sheriff directly. I won't be dismissed by some deputy. If the man's going to shirk his duty, I want him to tell me to my face." Margaret reached out to stroke her daughter's hair. "I may have to make a scene. I could even be arrested."

Faith was so angry she couldn't speak for a moment. She was being dismissed every time she turned around, first by Paul and now by her mother. Hadn't she been pulling her own weight, the same as anyone else? Didn't she spend the better part of her days helping Aunt Eva with this chore or that? Or fishing for the evening meal? Which, she noticed, her mother didn't mind eating.

Meanwhile, the look in Margaret's eyes told the whole story. She wasn't about to change her mind, or even listen to her daughter's complaints. The time for talking was over.

"Can I at least stay here with Aunt Eva?"

A blue jay called from a tree next to the charred remains of Red-Moon's barn, a single piercing note that hung in the room. Faith shifted her gaze from one adult face to another, from her mother's to Aunt Eva's to Ben's to Winona's and Judson's.

"Well?" she asked.

"I'm not sure it's safe here," Margaret said.

"Safe?"

"Look, honey," Aunt Eva cut in, "someone tried to kill Red-Moon. I don't know what exactly went wrong. Maybe Red-Moon moved at the last minute, or maybe the shooter lost his nerve. However it happened, the man who shot Red-Moon likely ran away thinkin' Red-Moon was dead. He knows better by now. He knows Red-Moon's alive, but unconscious and—"

Faith finished her aunt's sentence. "And he can't let Red-Moon wake up."

"I wouldn't go that far," Ben said. "Any low-down dog who'd shoot a defenseless old man has gotta be a coward. So maybe he's hidin' in his house, just hopin' that Red-Moon dies before wakin' up. But it could be the other way 'round. It could be he'll come back to finish the job."

Faith stared down at her feet for a moment. She was out of choices and every argument that came to mind was useless. And there was something else, something that hadn't been said. Most likely, the adults believed the words didn't need saying, but Faith decided to speak up anyway.

"Mom, you're going into Stroudsburg. Ben, you and Mr. Crow are going out to search for Paul. Mrs. Crow, you're going home in case Paul returns. That leaves Aunt Eva by herself."

The silence that fell upon them, heavy as a shroud, was broken only by the rushing wind. At another time, Aunt Eva would be worried about a crop-killing frost. The corn was only a foot high and the beans were newly planted. Not now, though. Now she had other things on her mind.

"If you go into Red-Moon's bedroom," she told her grandniece, "you'll find a shotgun leanin' against the dresser." Aunt Eva took Faith's hand. "Maybe I'm past my prime, but there was a day when I hunted ducks and geese right alongside my husband. Now, I'm not one to brag on myself, but I brought home our dinner more than once. You don't need to worry about me."

Nineteen

DON'T WORRY? FAITH Covington was starting to think that all the Lenape community did was worry. Every day was a new struggle. What if the resorts close down? What if there's a late frost and I lose my crop? What if I don't have any luck come hunting season? What if there's a drought and the plants in the forest stop growing? What if a blizzard tears a hole in my roof? What if the chickens get sick and stop laying eggs? There was no end to their fears.

Faith left Aunt Eva's house and walked across the yard to the fence surrounding the garden. Another worry. Drawn by the prospect of a fine meal, some small animal—probably a woodchuck—had managed to dig under the chicken-wire fence. Aunt Eva hadn't begrudged the animal, though she would almost surely have killed the creature if it had forgotten how to get out again. Now the bottom edge of the fence would have to be reburied.

A gust of wind lifted Faith's hair as she knelt down to assess the damage. What had happened was obvious enough. A large rock, heaved up by a winter frost, had pushed the chicken wire close to the surface. Somehow, the woodchuck had discovered the weak point and taken advantage. Anywhere else and the creature would need to dig down a foot before getting through.

If Paul were here, Faith thought, *he'd surely claim that the animal's spirit guide led it to the right spot.* Hoping to trick him, she'd once asked Paul if the mosquito biting his neck had a spirit guide. Paul's response was as quick as it was serious. Mosquitoes—and many other malignant creatures, like flies—were agents of the *Mahtantu*, the Evil One, who delighted in tormenting the People.

"Well, how come the good spirits don't keep this *Mahtantu* away?"

"They tried when the *Mahtantu* first appeared, but he was too powerful."

At that point, Faith had given up. You couldn't argue with Paul. He held to his own beliefs without feeling the least need to convince anyone else of their truth. Paul wasn't out to make converts. His goal was only to probe deeper into the realm of the spirits. Just as he'd told her on the day they met, finding his spirit guide was the great task that dominated his dreams. Until he achieved that goal, he would be lost in confusion.

Faith's owl chose that moment to fly across the yard, gliding on silent wings to perch in a tree thirty feet away. She wasn't surprised—the bird seemed to have adopted her—only this time it wasn't alone. A pair of crows followed. The crows were all black: black eyes, black wings, black beaks, black tails. Intent on menacing their ancient enemy, they swooped in, the tips of their wing feathers separated like the fingers of a hand, veering away only at the very last second. The owl appeared not to notice. It remained unmoving, its eyes focused on Faith Covington.

"What do you want?" Faith hesitated a minute before speaking again. "Oh, not talking this afternoon? Crow's got your tongue?" She turned back to her work, finally managing to push the edge of the shovel beneath the rock. The crows were calling to each other as they menaced the owl, their relentless caws filling the small open space in the forest until Faith finally looked up to find the owl's eyes burning into her back. Then she rose to her feet and walked across the yard, waving the shovel. That was enough for the crows. They flew off, hugging the treetops, their indignant screams gradually fading. But the owl, except for a quick flutter of its wings, failed to react.

"Not going anywhere?" Faith lowered the shovel to the ground. "If you've got something to tell me, why don't you just say it?"

The bird remained silent and Faith stared into its eyes for a moment before returning to her chores. She finished the job of burying the fence then entered the garden and began to weed the mounds, careful to avoid the pale bean sprouts. When she finally broke for lunch at eleven o'clock, the sun, directly overhead, was a ball of gold in a cloudless sky so intensely blue it might have been freshly painted by the Master Creator himself.

Faith brought her tools, her shovel and hoe, to Aunt Eva's shed and put them inside. Then she gathered an armful of wood and headed inside. She was hungry and the remains of white beans from a dinner earlier in the week, stowed in Aunt Eva's tiny fridge, beckoned to her. Quickly, she made a fire in the stove and placed the pot on one of the burners. She thought mostly of Paul while she turned the beans with a long wooden spoon. Was he home? Or at Red-Moon's? Or still out in the forest, intent on his mission?

Not having a telephone was driving her crazy and Faith decided to risk a quick trip to Red-Moon's before dinner.

She could avoid the road by canoeing past the small island with the beaver's lodge. If she got there before dark and only stayed for a minute, how much danger would she really be in?

Faith washed the dishes after lunch then walked out to the lake. Instantly, she realized that her canoe plan was off the table. Whitecaps broke the surface of the water from one shore to another. Paddling a canoe into the face of a stiff breeze was an art she'd yet to master. Without Paul to help, whatever way she tried to go, the wind would spin the canoe around and push it back across the water. She might follow the wind, of course, if it happened to be blowing in the right direction. In this case, however, the wind was blowing in her face. She wouldn't get ten feet without being forced back to shore.

Usually, the lake served Faith as a refuge. Not today. Even the waterfowl, the geese and the ducks, had retreated to the water's edge. Faith watched a small heron moving through the reeds at the edge of the island twenty feet away. Wind or no wind, life went on. She thought of her father, stalking a job, perhaps in one of New York's skyscrapers, the Woolworth Building, or even the newly constructed Empire State Building, the tallest building in the world. Had his job interview gone well, or had he been rejected as he'd been rejected so many times over the past few months? If Aunt Eva had a telephone, Faith would already know. But they were completely isolated—not just Faith, alone in Aunt Eva's house—but the entire community. Only a week ago, their self-reliance had seemed a benefit. Now Faith wasn't sure. Forces beyond your control, powerful forces, could run over your life no matter where or how you lived. Run over your life like a city bus over a centipede.

Suddenly, Faith smiled, remembering Paul's *Mahtantu*, his Evil One. Maybe the *Mahtantu* had sent the Depression.

FINDING FAITH

The *Mahtantu* was behind the occasional droughts that killed the People's crops and left them starving in the winter. At his command, the fish stopped biting and the flies started. Every illness could be laid on his doorstep. So why not the Depression?

Faith made her way back to the house, pushing her way through the wind-whipped branches of the pines blocking her way. Fishing was pretty much out; she could no more cast a line into the face of the wind than she could paddle a canoe. Of course, there was still the garden, half of which had yet to be weeded, but Faith hadn't gotten more than a few hours sleep the night before and she was too tired to work. Too tired and too anxious. She decided, instead, to read. Fetching her book, *Cimarron*, along with a rocking chair from the kitchen, she lugged both into the sun-flooded yard. Then she went back inside to find a coat. She chose one of Aunt Eva's, a corduroy jacket with a flannel lining that fell to her hips.

Before she came to the lake, Faith had been enjoying her novel. *Cimarron* had been a huge best-seller just a few years before. According to *Variety*, Edna Ferber had sold the movie rights to her book for $125,000. That was more than most families could hope to earn in several lifetimes. Nevertheless, now that she'd lived for a time among the People, Faith was having trouble with the book. *Cimarron* was about the white settlers who flooded into the Oklahoma territory fifty years ago. They let nothing stand in their way, least of all a strip of the territory granted to the Cherokee Indians when they were expelled from Georgia. The land had been guaranteed to them by a treaty signed in 1828, when nobody except the Cherokee wanted to live there. Unfortunately, the land had become valuable to cattle ranchers by 1889 when Oklahoma was opened up to homesteaders. The Cherokees had to go.

What would Paul make of this? Not much, probably. He was a lot more interested in spirit guides than a history that kept repeating itself. Unlike Aunt Eva, he never seemed bitter.

Faith set the book at her feet. At any moment, she expected Paul to emerge from the depths of the forest as though produced by a magician's sleight of hand. Funny thing, but you never knew what direction Paul would come from, only that he'd appear without warning, silent as a ghost.

That last thought made her shiver. What in the world could Paul be up to? Almost a full day had gone by with no sign of him. He must have known how worried his parents would be, how every minute increased their fears. If he hadn't yet returned, something—or someone—must be preventing him. Of course, he might be at home right now, explaining to his mother, or he might have been found by his father and Ben. Judson Crow had been mad as a hornet this morning. If he happened to run across his son wandering through the woods, a moment of reckoning would surely follow, a well-deserved moment of reckoning. The community had enough problems without Paul adding to their worries.

Suddenly exhausted, Faith began to drift off. She closed her eyes, her chin gradually dropping to her chest. From a great distance, an owl called, over and over—*hoo, hoo, hooooooo*—its cries borne across the heavens by the sharp wind. Faith felt herself drawn not to the animal, but to the river of moving air that carried its lonesome cries.

Without warning, Faith's body seemed to dissolve and she rose above the trees. She was soaring now, each second bringing her closer to Paul. At last she understood the owl and why it had come to her. The bird was not her spirit guide, but Paul's, its mission to protect him from harm. He was in trouble, trouble he could not escape by himself, and saving him was her job. That was the owl's message, that was why she'd come to the mountain in the first place. The only problem was that she didn't know where he was and the wind was taking her further and further away, carrying her across land and sea, past the moon and the stars...

Faith awakened with a start. The owl was perched at the edge of the forest, its look especially stern. The same breeze stirring Faith's hair rippled through its long feathers. Faith found herself wanting to turn away, but she couldn't shake the belief that Paul was in serious trouble and that it was up to her to do something about it. All the rest of her dream had vanished. Gravity had reclaimed her body. Soaring was no longer a possibility; soaring was for the birds.

For a long moment, Faith leaned back in the rocking chair, her eyes closed, and listened to the forest sounds, the rattling of tree branches, the moan of the wind through a little stand of long-needled pines, the call of a songbird concealed in the trees. Only gradually did another sound, this one far from natural, intrude. A car was making its way along the road.

Faith leapt up, seized by a sudden dread. One part of her mind insisted that the vehicle probably belonged to Ben or one of the other Indians. It might even be Sheriff Garber, coming at her mother's insistence to right every wrong. But somehow she couldn't make herself believe that help was on the way. In the movies, when the cavalry arrived, it was to attack—not to protect—the Indians.

Faith looked across the yard at the owl. The animal continued to stare at her for a moment before rising almost straight up, the beat of its long wings steady and powerful. The bird's yellow eyes remained fixed on her until it cleared the treetops and swung around to fly into the depths of the forest.

A moment later, a car emerged from around the bend—Abe Hoskins' Oldsmobile sedan. The constable wasn't driving, though. Crease Marron sat behind the wheel, his head swiveling back and forth until his gaze fell on Faith. Then he brought the sedan to a stop and set the parking brake.

Taking his time, Marron lowered the window. "What's your name, girl?" he asked.

"Faith Covington."

"Where's your mother?"

"She's not here."

"Don't sass me, girl. I didn't ask you where she wasn't. I asked you where she was." Marron tugged at a lock of his unruly hair, his eyes turning inward. The inflamed scar on his cheek formed a jagged red line that disappeared behind his ear. "Hear tell," he finally said, "that your momma was at the train station this mornin'. Hear tell she bought herself a ticket to Stroudsburg. Musta been right important if she left you all by your lonesome."

Faith didn't trust herself to speak. She was too angry, and too afraid. Margaret Covington's whereabouts, not to mention her intentions, were none of Crease Marron's business. Nevertheless, he seemed awfully agitated…and Abe Hoskins wasn't around to rein him in.

"Well, you gonna answer me?"

"No, I'm not."

"Is that right?" When Faith didn't reply, Marron said, "One thing I can't abide is a papoose with a sassy mouth. Come over here, girl."

"No, I won't. You have no right to order me around."

Marron laughed. "Well, in that case, I'll just have to come to you." He opened the door and put a leg on the ground then hesitated for a moment, as if reconsidering. Finally, he stepped out of the car.

Faith's fear drained away as Marron rose to his full height—her fear but not her anger. She wanted to meet his threat with force, but that was out of the question. At age thirteen, there was only one course of action open to her and she took it, spinning on her heel and dashing into the forest.

Twenty

THE FOREST TOOK Faith Covington in as a monastery in some ancient land might take in a lost and hungry traveler. She felt instantly safe, instantly protected. Faith was familiar with most of the trails near the farm and she flew along a series of paths that zigzagged between the rocks and trees. Behind her, Crease Marron was trying to force his way through the tangle of trees and brush. Between curses, he threatened her with a "whippin'" she'd "never forget."

Faith remembered someone, probably Aunt Eva, claiming that the original settlers never learned the ways of the forest, that they hated the wilderness and wished only to clear the forest away. Crease Marron might have been a case in point. Though he'd lived on the mountain all his life, the forest was not his friend. Second by second, he fell further and further behind.

Faith stopped running after a few minutes, choosing to conceal herself in a thick grove of young hemlocks. Invisible, she listened with amusement to Crease Marron's fumbling attempts to catch her. Everything Paul had told her about the forest came flooding back. Flooding back as the sunlight flooded down through the branches of the hemlocks to fall across her head and shoulders.

Marron didn't last long. Not more than fifteen minutes passed before Faith heard the Oldsmobile start up and move down the road. At that point, she abandoned her hiding place. But instead of returning to Aunt Eva's, she headed deeper into the forest. She didn't know exactly where she was going, but she was sure she was safer in the woods than back at the farm. There was also Paul to think about.

The sun was still high enough to cast its light through the trees and onto the dried leaves carpeting the forest floor. The wind remained strong as well, twisting the branches so that the pattern of light and shadow was in constant movement. Never in her life had Faith felt so complete. She made steady progress skirting the Graveyard and the Schnozz, until she eventually reached the small pond where she and Aunt Eva had dug for swamp potatoes, the one with the hundreds of irises.

What had Aunt Eva called them? Blue flag, that was it. Well, the irises were past their prime, their blossoms shriveled into indigo ribbons. They'd been replaced by thousands of newly grown lily pads. Intensely green, the lily pads were no more than a few inches across; they rested, placid and motionless, on the surface of the pond, but Faith wasn't fooled. They were fighting, each of them, for precious space. Eventually, they would throw off huge white blossoms; eventually they would make the seed that ensured their survival. Assuming they weren't crowded out, assuming they lived that long.

Shadows moved beneath the lily pads—gray shadows no longer than Faith's little finger. Fish, perhaps, or tadpoles growing into frogs. According to Paul, frogs' legs were a staple during the hot summer months when they were hunted at night with the use of flashlights. Frogs were also served in French restaurants in New York, the expensive ones she'd rarely visited, even when the family was doing well.

Faith stopped and crouched down, allowing her mind to drift back to the city, to the hustle and bustle of Manhattan. The clamor of the city reached out to her—the crash of the subways, the constant ebb and flow of the traffic, the murmur of conversation on the crowded sidewalks, the harsh cries of the newsboys hawking the evening papers. Here, on the mountain, all sound was delivered by a wind split into a thousand parts as it rose and fell, as it moved through the leaves of a honey locust or the needles of a pine or the dense woody brush at the far edge of the pond. As it rushed past her own ears and whistled in her hair.

She closed her eyes, reaching for something that had eluded her for days. There was a life here, a life beyond all the many individual lives, the trees or the grasses, the lily pads or the little creatures that lived beneath them, beyond even her own life. Suddenly, without deciding to, she jumped to her feet. Instinctively, she looked around for her owl, but the bird was nowhere to be found.

Where would Paul go? That was the question, right? All along she'd felt a need to rescue Paul. Which was stupid, she'd told herself, because he might not even be in trouble. But just as she couldn't rid herself of the impulse, she now found herself asking the logical follow-up questions. Where did he go? Where should she start?

Faith had decided that playing detective was for Nancy Drew, a character newly introduced into girl's literature. Nancy was rich; she had time to spare. But Faith didn't have time. She would have to go back to Aunt Eva's that night, preferably in the early evening before her mother returned. And before the sun set, too. Right this minute, with the sun pouring down, courage was easy to come by. The forest was far more mysterious at night, more mysterious and more threatening.

Faith finally decided to revisit the mine. Paul had been very interested in that mine and it was only a short distance away. And there was the road, too, just a half-mile beyond it. That was where Paul found the surveyor's pole. Maybe he'd gone to the road and been seen.

A hundred yards from the mine, which lay beyond an outcropping of gray rock, Faith stopped in her tracks at the sound of men engaged in loud conversation. Fortunately, she'd taken her time, approaching the mine as silently as possible, though nowhere near as silently as Paul. Not that she would likely have been heard in any event. The three men, Faith discovered when she crept closer, were too involved in an ongoing argument to hear anything but the sound of their own voices.

Jaspin Gore's voice was the loudest. He stood with his back to Faith, a bored Abe Hoskins to his left. Opposite Gore, a middle-aged man, his canvas pants held up with leather suspenders, shook his head in exasperation.

"Sorry, Jaspin, I just can't tell you what you want to hear."

"Now, you listen to me, McGregor. When I hire a geologist, I expect a straight answer."

"I've given you all the answers I'm prepared to give," McGregor replied. He didn't seem at all afraid of Gore, although he was a much smaller man. "There's coal here, yes. Enough to be commercially feasible? Probably, but not certainly. In any event, the coal is close to the surface. You can strip it away without digging any deep mines."

"That's not good enough. As you can see, there's no road. I'd not only have to foot the costs of building one, the considerable costs, I'd also have to convince the state legislature in Harrisburg to grant me a right-of-way because the road would cross a nature preserve. I can't justify the expense or the effort on a *probably*."

McGregor smiled, revealing a set of large, stained teeth. He reached into the pockets of his trousers with both hands, withdrawing a pipe and a pouch of tobacco, undoubtedly the source of the stains. In no apparent hurry, he filled the pipe to the brim before lighting up.

"What you need to think about, Jaspin, is how much worse it'd be if I told you there was a huge seam of coal right under our feet and I turned out to be wrong."

"Don't tell me what I need to think about. You work for me and—"

"Oh, no, I don't." McGregor's voice was calm and relaxed. He sucked slowly at the pipe stem then puffed out a cloud of smoke. "I have my own company. I work for no man and I'm not at your beck and call. You'll have my written report, along with an invoice for my services, on your desk within forty-eight hours. What you do after that is your own business."

With that, McGregor turned on his heel and marched off. Jaspin Gore shouted after him. "It was you who came to me, McGregor, with a story about coal on the Pocono plateau. Don't you walk away now!"

Abe Hoskins shook his head in disgust. "This ain't goin' like you said, Mr. Gore. First Red-Moon's barn, then Red-Moon? This here is a heap more trouble than I signed on for. I sure hope it ain't for nothin'."

"I don't know a thing about what happened to Red-Moon. Don't care, neither. But I'll tell you this. A coal strike up here, this close to the railroad, would be worth millions. I don't intend to give that up because some Indian got into a fight."

That said, Jaspin Gore strode off into the brush, chasing after the geologist. Hoskins dutifully followed. Faith almost felt sorry for him. She wondered if Hoskins had found a spirit guide, or if he lived with the confusion Paul spoke about. Hoskins was an Indian, after all, an Indian who'd chosen an independent path. To Jaspin Gore, though, he was little more than a servant. She supposed all of them were.

A few minutes later, Faith heard a car start up and drive off. When a second car followed, she listened until it could no longer be heard, until the only sound to reach her ears was the relentless moan of the wind. Then she approached the mine, peered into the dark tunnel and shivered. The timbers securing the sides and roof looked old enough to crumble and there was rock piled up twenty feet away, obviously the result of a partial cave-in. More to the point, several sets of footprints marred the thick layers of dust and dirt on the tunnel floor.

Much as she didn't want to, Faith had to admit the truth. This would be a perfect place to hide a kidnapped child, or even a body. There were no houses within miles and the nearest road was a ribbon of asphalt running through dense forest. There wasn't even the sort of trail that hunters used to get in and out of the forest. Most likely, before Jaspin Gore sent his geologist and his surveyors, no one had visited the mine for years and years. No one except Paul Crow.

Faith took a step then shivered and said, "Paul?" Her voice echoed in the closed space, mocking her. Surely, if he was here, Paul would be gagged, his mouth bound with tape or something to keep him from yelling for help. Maybe that was why Marron had come looking for her. Maybe he suspected that she'd been to the mine with Paul. She took another step, this time closing her eyes, which only made it worse, and shouted Paul's name. The echo was even stronger, but Faith thought she heard something, a quick flurry of movement that vanished a second later.

Sighing, Faith told herself to think. She shoved her hands into her pockets, her right hand closing around a small box of kitchen matches. Probably, she'd jammed the matches into her pocket when she lit a fire in the stove before lunch. But so what? Was she supposed to explore the mine, lighting matches as she went, holding them until they burned her fingers? That was for the movies, where matches stayed lit for minutes at a time. What she needed was a torch.

The first step was to find a length of wood dry enough to burn freely. Green wood, like the branch of a living tree, was out. Too full of moisture. Even dead branches lying on the damp ground wouldn't do. But the long-discarded handle of the pickaxe she found lying ten feet inside the dry tunnel was perfect. Assuming she could build a fire hot enough to ignite the wood.

Faith began with a patch of tall grass that had died in the fall. The nearly white stalks had the feathery remains of the plant's seed at their ends and were dry enough to crackle when she molded them into a loose ball. She laid the ball on the ground, walked over to a dead bush, and broke off a handful of twigs and branches. She arranged the twigs in a pyramid over the ball of grass, and then created a second, larger pyramid with the branches.

One match. That was Paul's motto. One fire, one match. Faith took a match from the pack and slid it along the striker. Then she thrust the yellow flame into the center of the dried grass. Instantly, the grass burst into flame, igniting the twigs within seconds. The branches took a bit longer, but when they finally began to burn, she added more, slightly larger branches, until she had a steady fire going. Then she balanced the wooden handle on two rocks, leaving one end to hang a few inches above the flames.

As she worked, Faith constantly monitored her surroundings. The fire was small, but the steady breeze would carry the odor out toward the road. The thick handle was taking forever to ignite and she had to add fuel several times before the handle burst into flame.

Faith left the handle in the fire long after it finally ignited, until the wood glowed red hot beneath the flames. Then she lifted the torch above her head and approached the mine. *Okay,* she told herself, *time to get going; this torch won't burn forever.* Unfortunately, her feet weren't listening. The depths of the mine remained darker than the darkest night. Anything might be down there, waiting for a human foolish enough to enter.

Faith shut her eyes, which was really foolish when she thought about it. The mine had to be searched and she needed to grow up. There were no goblins or ghosts or trolls or ogres lurking in the gloom. There were no bad guys, either, or they would have responded when she called Paul's name. If anyone, or anything, was alive and living in the depths of the mine, it was Paul Crow.

The little pep talk worked, but the message was entirely wrong. Faith walked, the torch held just above her head, for no more than thirty feet before the bats clinging to the roof of the tunnel began to stir. Five steps later, the animals were in full flight. Instinctively, they headed for the mouth of the mine, hundreds of them, passing within inches of Faith's head and body. So close that the warm breeze kicked up by their wings washed over her like the breath of a huge, hungry animal.

Forgetting the need for silence, Faith screamed at the top of her lungs and dove into the dirt. She held the torch above her head, swinging it back and forth like a sword. And she kept swinging the torch, on her knees, gasping for breath, her heart pounding wildly, for minutes after the silhouette of the last bat disappeared into the sunlight beyond the mouth of the mine.

Somehow, Faith managed to stand. Somehow, though she was shivering, she forced herself to go forward. All for nothing, as it turned out. Faith followed the tunnel for nearly fifty yards, until she came upon a heap of shiny coal, recently dug by the look of it. There were footprints all around the pile but none further on. Paul was not there.

Faith didn't waste a moment. She retraced her steps, emerging from the mineshaft into the sunlight to draw a deep breath. Then she put out the torch and the little fire, covering both with dirt. Her heart continued to pound away, as the little hairs on the back of her neck remained erect. She scanned the forest and listened for the sound of an approaching car, but the bats were long gone and the only sound was the sound of the wind. The wind rushed into her ears, filling them with a hollow roar. She could not seem to catch her breath.

Now what? Unsummoned, the question popped into her mind, breaking through her panicked state, forcing her to think. She'd gone down the tunnel hoping to find Paul. What she found, instead, was a big nothing. Somebody had been inside the tunnel long enough to dig a small amount of coal, but that somebody was not Paul Crow. Now what?

With no ready answer, Faith began to walk around the clearing, mostly because she was still too energized to stay in one place. A memory of Paul emerged as she made her way along the edge of the forest. They were out on the lake one evening with the bats flying around them. Faith was frightened because the little animals sometimes passed within inches of her, but not Paul Crow. Bats, Paul explained, were spirits from the underworld. Not hell, but a place where humans who mistreated others were sent to atone upon their deaths. A portion of that atonement allowed their release on summer nights to eat the insects that tormented the People.

Faith shuddered. For just a second, there in the tunnel, she'd believed, completely and utterly, that the bats were about to eat a human named Faith Covington. Maybe as punishment for her invasion of their underworld.

Minutes passed before Faith regained the ability to focus her attention, and only then because the shotgun shell lying at her feet was bright red. Paul, she remembered, almost always wore a leather vest over his shirt, a vest made for him by Aunt Eva. Trimmed with blue feathers, the deer hide vest had a row of loops that ran across the front, which Paul used to hold spare shells for his shotgun.

Faith was certain those shells were red, like the shell on the ground. But so what? Maybe all shotgun shells were red. Faith picked up the shell and examined it carefully. She didn't find Paul's name anywhere, but the words *Remington .20 gauge* engraved on the bottom of the shell, the metal part, caught her attention.

According to Paul, the shotgun he carried wasn't meant for large animals like deer. Raccoons, porcupines, rabbits, squirrels, he'd explained, that's what the weapon was designed for. Then he'd gone on to say something about gauge, something unusual.

Faith nodded to herself as she remembered. According to Paul, the higher the gauge, the weaker the shotgun. Just the opposite of pistols and rifles. Deer were usually hunted with twelve-gauge shotguns. Birds and smaller animals with sixteen- and twenty-gauge shotguns.

Alright, Faith admitted, *Paul's been here*. But she already knew that. The truth was that he might have dropped the shell on any number of occasions. On the other hand, if this spot wasn't the starting point for his disappearance, finding him seemed about as likely as Abe Hoskins deciding to enforce the laws he'd sworn to uphold.

Suddenly drained, Faith sat down with her back to the trunk of a white oak. *Think*, she told herself. *Who took Paul? Where was he taken?* Neither Jaspin Gore nor Abe Hoskins had mentioned Paul. And neither appeared to be involved in the attack on Red-Moon. So, who did that leave? Crease Marron? But, no, Marron didn't live in the community. He'd need a car to get to Red-Moon's, which meant Red-Moon would have heard him coming. This wasn't New York, with thousands and thousands of cars on the streets. On the mountain, the sound of a car engine attracted immediate attention.

The question remained: If not Jaspin Gore or Abe Hoskins or Crease Marron, then who? The answer jumped up and smacked her on the face. Caleb Littlewolf was the last man standing. He might easily have traveled from his own place to Red-Moon's farm without being seen, might have lurked in the forest, concealed, until an opportunity presented itself.

Faith looked around the small clearing as she considered what to do next. Her mother, of course, would insist that the matter be placed in the hands of some adult, Aunt Eva, say, or Ben. The other option—to personally confront the man who kidnapped Paul and attempted to murder Red-Moon—sounded ridiculous, even to her. And yet...and yet she had to do something.

Faith rose to her feet and took a final look around. That was when a road, or what remained of it after a hundred years, finally caught her attention.

Twenty-One

WHAT FAITH COVINGTON saw was a slight depression, overgrown with trees and brush, on the far side of the mine. It was no more than ten feet wide and two feet deep. She might have missed it altogether—in fact, she almost had, though she'd been to this spot before—if the channel wasn't so regular. Varying neither in width nor depth, it cut a straight line for a hundred yards before curving around an outcropping or rock. And that struck her as really weird. Straight lines simply played no part in nature's plan. That's why it was so easy to get lost in the forest. Even the paths created by animals twisted and turned so many times you didn't know whether you were coming or going.

Something else occurred to Faith as she stood in the shade of the oak, something equally obvious. A long time ago, maybe as long as a hundred years, somebody had dug this mine. Whoever that somebody was, he surely wouldn't dig a mine unless there was a handy road. The Covingtons had burned coal in their little fireplace in New York on many a winter's night and Faith could personally testify to the fuel's weight. A century ago, any significant amount of coal would have been hauled away in horse-drawn wagons. Running wagons through a forest was a clear impossibility. There must have been a road and she was looking at what remained of it.

Faith nodded to herself as she checked her surroundings. Maybe she'd been tentative before, doubting herself every step of the way, but she wasn't doubting herself now. She was more focused than she'd ever been in her life—and, for once, she felt like the forest was showing her the way. The only real issue was whether the road connected to someone's home or another road, or if it simply petered out. One good thing was that she didn't have to fear becoming lost. The path she intended to travel led right back to the mine.

By the time Faith took her first step, the sun, though still above the treetops, had fallen from its midday zenith and the sky was filmed by high, lacy clouds. The wind had slowed as well and now barely stirred the larger branches. Off to Faith's left, a bright orange chipmunk popped out from behind a low-growing shrub. The little animal stared at Faith for a moment then vanished so fast it might never have been there at all.

Faith smiled. One afternoon, before they went fishing, Paul declared that he could tame any chipmunk in less than an hour.

"Their spirits are very curious," he told her. "And very greedy."

To prove his point, he placed a shelled hickory nut next to an angled outcropping of gray rock. "The chipmunk's burrow is under the rock," he explained as he stepped back.

"How do you know that? I can't see any holes."

The chipmunk's head appeared before Paul could reply, seeming almost to come through the rock itself. The animal sniffed twice then snatched the nut and dragged it beneath the rock and into its burrow. Seconds later, the animal reappeared to find Paul holding a nut between his fingers.

"You see how greedy he is? No matter how much food he's stored away, he always wants more." Paul tossed the nut, very gently, so that it came to rest a few feet from the chipmunk. Once again, the little animal rose on its hind legs to sniff the air. Once again, it snatched up the nut and beat a hasty retreat.

By the fourth appearance, the chipmunk was taking the nut from Paul's hand. By the seventh, he was able to stroke the back of the animal's head.

If Paul could make an animal appear seemingly out of thin air, the least she could do was find her friend.

Faith made slower progress than she would have liked. What remained of the old road was easy enough to follow with her eye. Her feet, on the other hand, faced a different problem. Little more than a depression in the forest floor, the road was a natural trap for rain. Faith learned this fact the hard way after she stepped onto what she thought to be grass, only to sink—ankle-deep—into sticky brown mud. It was all she could do to get her foot out without losing her boot in the process.

Faith was forced to make her way along the edge of the ancient road, and her progress slowed to a crawl. The brush was thicker there, the trees closely packed. The detours along animal trails she would ordinarily have taken, the paths of least resistance, were unavailable now. She had to keep the road, which twisted and turned more often than she would have liked, in view at all times. At one point, Faith stumbled into a patch of half-grown blackberry vines. The thorns dug into her clothes and into the skin on her hands and wrists, deep enough to draw blood when she staggered out of the thicket. At another point, the road disappeared into a swampy pond. It wasn't designed that way, of course. A hundred years before, when the road was first built, the land had surely been dry. Not anymore.

Faith had to make her way around the marsh, her route blocked by trees and brush and rocky outcropping that rose above her head. She nearly became lost in the process, only stumbling on the road entirely by accident, and only a moment before she panicked altogether. She had no idea where she was, none. But she did know that if she got lost, she might never find her way home. Every year, according to Aunt Eva, some tourist wandered too far into the woods and died of exposure. In fact, sometimes their bodies were never found.

Faith sat at the edge of the road. Her heart was drumming against her ribs like a trapped animal trying to break free of its cage and her clothes were soiled from top to bottom. A long scratch, oozing blood at either end, marred the side of her neck. Faith ignored all of this, her eye suddenly taken with a patch of mud only a few yards away. The mud was dry on the surface and deceptively smooth. The man who'd stepped directly into it, for example, had surely been fooled. The hole he left behind was six inches deep.

Careful where she placed her feet, Faith moved close enough to examine the area before and behind the muddy patch. The impressions she found were faint—though Paul, undoubtedly, would have picked them up in a flash—but they were definitely there. She found them in the broken stalk of an orange hawkweed, a crushed dandelion, the flattened tips of the finer grasses.

Slowly at first, Faith began to follow the trail. She tried, as much as possible, to move from rock to rock as she made her way, but when there were no rocks available, she tested the ground with every step. The effort paid off ten minutes later when she discovered a pair of blue feathers dangling from the needle of a budding hawthorn. Paul's vest was trimmed with blue jay feathers.

Faith tucked the feathers into the breast pocket of her coveralls. If she didn't find Paul, at least she could prove that he'd come this way. One thing had become clear: Paul wasn't alone. There were two sets of footprints in the muddier sections. One set was made by a smooth sole, surely Paul's moccasins. The second was made by the treads of a man's boots.

Distracted for a moment when a pair of screaming crows flew overhead, Faith slowed to a stop. She somehow expected the owl to follow the crows—or maybe she was just hoping. But the owl apparently had business elsewhere and the cawing of the crows grew more and more faint as they made their way above the treetops. The sun had dropped a little further now and the larger trees threw long, dense shadows that stretched on and on. Faith had a choice to make. If she started right now, she'd probably reach RedMoon's home or Aunt Eva's farm before dark. Aunt Eva and Ben would surely know what to do next, especially if they were familiar with the ancient road and where it came out.

But what if the road was unknown to them? What if she had to lead them back to the mine in the morning, if the road had to be tracked all over again? How much time did Paul have, for goodness sake? For all Faith knew, he might already be…

Faith didn't allow herself to finish the sentence. She stared out along the road, willing herself to think. The end of the road she was following might be a hundred yards away and it might be ten miles. She might reach the end in fifteen minutes. She might walk all night and still have miles to go. Worst of all, the road might end in the middle of nowhere, leaving her to make her way back in the dark or to wait for morning.

Faith pulled her jacket tight around her. The wind had picked up and the few lazy clouds that hazed the sun had vanished. With the sun dropping in the west, the atmosphere was rapidly cooling. Later tonight, it would be downright cold.

She took a step, then another, then finally continued on. The way she saw it, there really was no choice.

The going was still slow, the footing still treacherous, but she persisted until she came upon an obstacle too big to ignore. A giant beech tree had fallen across the road. Seventy feet long, its branches rose into the air, a miniature forest of their own, while its twisted white roots, torn from the ground, projected from the end of the trunk like the tentacles of a giant squid.

Faith's eyes shifted to the right and the left, searching for the easiest way around the tree. She thought, at first, that she might climb over the middle, but the trunk was awfully thick. No, best to detour around the upper part. On the other end, the torn roots had left a hole in the ground that was certain to be filled with water. The last thing she needed was to fight her way through another swamp.

A noise from behind the fallen tree, a low huff, almost of exasperation, cut through Faith's thoughts, banishing them to some dark corner of her mind. A head appeared beyond the trunk, a great shaggy head, followed by the shoulders and body of an eastern black bear. The bear rose on its hind legs, its wet black nose twitching madly. A low growl rumbled up from its gigantic chest.

Faith started to turn, her first instinct to run, but checked herself. Running was the worst thing she could do. Or so Paul had told her—and she believed him. Escape was for prey animals and a predator's first instinct was to chase anything that moved. Besides, Faith was sick of all the nonsense, of the many obstacles, of her own fearful thoughts. She snatched up a branch and waved it above her head like a flag. The bear pulled back, its nose still twitching, then dropped onto all fours behind the trunk. A second later, the creature rose again, its head turning right and left until one tiny eye fastened on Faith.

The bear huffed twice, a breathy sound that revealed not a threat, but the animal's obvious confusion.

"*Huff* yourself." Faith waved the branch, hoping it made her look bigger than she was. "You're blocking my way."

The bear froze at the sound of Faith's voice. Then, as if the animal had at last figured out who and what she was, it dropped onto all fours and moved off into the forest, taking its time, making no effort to be silent.

Faith dropped the branch and took a deep breath before resuming her journey. Though she could only imagine what would have happened if she'd climbed over the trunk of the fallen tree, only to land in the bear's lap, she was unafraid. All thought of turning back had vanished. She would see her quest through to the end, no matter where this road led her. After all, wasn't that exactly what she'd been doing since she and her mother got on the train?

From a great distance, she heard the call of an owl, its lonesome cry somehow confirming her judgment.

Twenty-Two

FAITH COVINGTON DIDN'T realize she'd come to the end of the road until she finally slipped through a cluster of half-grown birch trees to encounter a light so dazzling that she jammed her eyes shut. Instinctively, she stepped back into the shadows and dropped to one knee before opening her eyes again. The contrast between the shadowy forest and the view from the edge of the little hill where she crouched was simply amazing, and not only the clearing with its small house and two smaller outbuildings. Beyond the trees at the far side of the house, the waters of Wildwood Lake caught the rays of the late-afternoon sun in the foam of its whitecaps and split them into millions of glittering shards. The lake appeared to be on fire.

Far from enchanted, what Faith felt at that moment was a powerful sense of relief. She'd done it; she'd tracked the ancient road to its very end. Where had she found the strength? The prim and proper young lady who dutifully attended Schuyler Academy, every hair in place, her dress without a wrinkle, shoes brightly polished? That girl would never have persevered through the mud and brambles and the briars, much less have dealt with the bear. The bear would have sent the old Faith running for her life.

But this was a new Faith. *And* a new life.

You'd think, Faith finally told herself, *between the bear and the mud and the briars and the thickets, that I've done enough for one day.* Meanwhile, she'd only gotten started and knew she had better remain on full alert. Bears were dangerous, true, but not as dangerous as certain human beings. Just ask Red-Moon.

Sighing, Faith shrugged off her exhaustion. The birch trees she was crouching behind offered scant cover. If someone came out of the house, she'd be spotted in a short minute. Faith didn't know exactly what she was going to do next, but she was sure she needed time to think about it. And a safe place in which to do her thinking. She found that refuge in the shadows of a blue spruce. The tree's branches, with their long, silver needles, swept to the ground, while a tangle of sow thistle at the edge of the clearing, alive with bright yellow flowers, further shielded her. From her position, lying prone, Faith was virtually invisible.

Faith first attempted to orient herself. The three buildings rising from the little clearing were unknown to her, but the configuration was familiar enough. A small house, a smaller barn, an even smaller tool shed. There was something missing, though, and it took Faith a moment to put her finger on the difference. Unlike all the homes she'd visited until then, whoever lived here had not planted a garden. Though farming was considered women's work, even Red-Moon planted corn and beans. Maybe he didn't care for the work, but hoeing weeds was a lot better than going hungry in the winter.

Here, too, an area had been set aside for a garden, but the plot was overgrown and the fence designed to protect the crops from small animals and deer had collapsed in several places. Faith at first thought that the homestead had been abandoned. But the house was in good repair and somebody had taken the time to run a mower across the grass and weeds in the yard. Whoever lived there had the money to buy food in both the summer and winter.

Faith registered the information without drawing any conclusions. Then she turned her attention to the road leading up to the property. Unpaved and filled with potholes and protruding rocks, the road had to be a continuation of the one running past Red-Moon's and Aunt Eva's. This was the end, though. The road stopped at the property line. Beyond, there was only the forest.

But, no, that wasn't exactly right, either. According to her mother, only a short stretch of forest separated the paved road serving the white community from the dirt road consigned to the Lenape. That would be very convenient for anyone who needed to communicate between the two communities.

Faith eased back a few yards and sat up, her attention caught by a commotion in the trees behind her. Mere streaks, a pair of gray squirrels chased each other at top speed through the branches of a hickory tree, a feat made all the more impressive by a steady breeze that shook the branches. From time to time, the squirrels came to an abrupt stop, the both of them, only their heads turning as they checked their surroundings. Even in the midst of their play, they were eternally vigilant.

She couldn't blame them. Squirrels were hunted by any number of animals—weasels, hawks, owls, bobcats. If a squirrel made a mistake, it wouldn't get a second chance. Faith felt the same way now.

Was Paul out there? Maybe in one of those two outbuildings. Or in the house, which appeared—at the moment—to be empty. Faith fought an urge to run across the yard and just start opening doors. The muscles in her legs had already tightened and she had to remind herself that she wasn't playing a game of hide-and-seek with her friends in New York. Somebody tried to kill Red-Moon and somebody took Paul. If she made a misstep, she would become victim number three.

Faith looked up in time to watch a familiar silhouette glide across the clearing to settle on the branch of tree. The owl became instantly immobile, a virtual statue as it merged with the shadows.

"So, you decided not to desert me," she whispered.

The owl didn't reply, and Faith turned back to her analysis. A second, very real possibility had suggested itself. She could work her way through the forest until she was out of sight then simply follow the dirt road to Red-Moon's house. The blue feathers tucked into her pocket were sure to catch her Aunt Eva's attention. And, of course, Aunt Eva would know who lived in the house. Faith was assuming the land belonged to Caleb Littlewolf, but that didn't have to be the case.

Faith's thoughts were interrupted by the sound of an approaching vehicle. She moved forward, propped on her elbows, just in time to watch a pickup truck stop in front of the house. Caleb Littlewolf emerged a moment later, his armed wrapped around a bag of groceries. Well, that settled that.

He walked onto his little porch and yanked open the unlocked front door. A dark blur flew out, darting between his legs—a big Labrador retriever. The dog turned circles in the yard, its tail thumping wildly.

Faith froze at the sight of the black lab. According to Aunt Eva, the People didn't keep dogs because they didn't want to chain them up. Littlewolf, unfortunately, wasn't playing by the People's rules. He cared about as much for the dog's spirit as for his overgrown garden.

"Dang you, dog, git back in the house."

The dog stopped running at the sound of his master's voice and began to sniff the air. It was only by mere luck that Faith was facing into the wind. If the wind were at her back, the dog would surely discover her by her scent. Even now, the animal seemed to sense that something was wrong. He took a few tentative steps in Faith's direction, but then Littlewolf grabbed the dog's collar and literally dragged him into the house.

"I swear, dog, if you don't start listenin', I'm gonna take you in the woods and shoot ya."

Faith took a deep breath when the door slammed shut then glanced over at the owl. Though it hadn't moved so much as an inch, it took her a long minute to find the bird, so lost was it in the shadows.

"Now what?" Faith whispered.

The answer came from within: *Wait.* But, no, that couldn't be right. Darkness would have no effect on the dog's hearing or his sense of smell. If she attempted to search the two small outbuildings—which was all she really could do unless Littlewolf went out again—the animal would surely detect her presence.

A moment later, a plume of smoke rose from a metal chimney on the roof. Caleb Littlewolf was preparing dinner. He wouldn't be going anywhere.

What I need to do, Faith told herself, *is get some help. Aunt Eva and Ben Hightower have guns. Judson Crow probably does, too. Could they force Littlewolf to submit to a search? Probably not.*

If Paul was hidden somewhere on the property, Littlewolf would have to fight. He wouldn't have any other choice.

Faith thought all of this through, yet she didn't go for help. In fact, she didn't move a muscle.

The setting sun was a glowing orange ball perched just above the treetops on the far side of the lake. In an hour, maybe an hour and a half, it would be completely dark. A full moon would rise later on. How much later? Faith was only sure there'd be enough time after sunset, an hour, at least, to check out the pair of outbuildings. That opportunity would end abruptly when the moon finally rose. There wasn't a cloud in the sky. The moonlight would be strong enough to cast shadows.

A flock of geese headed for the lake chose that moment to fly over the house. They were calling to each other, as they did whenever a flock landed or took off. This time, their raucous honking drove Caleb Littlewolf's dog into a frenzy. The animal barked and growled and literally threw itself at the door. Its master's reaction came an instant later.

"Will you hush up?" Littlewolf shouted, his voice carrying all the way to Faith a hundred yards away.

Though it yelped from time to time, apparently in response to its master's corrections, the dog didn't quiet until the geese settled down.

A thought began to form in Faith's mind, a thought that fled at the sound of an approaching car. Faith wasn't surprised when Abe Hoskins' Oldsmobile pulled up, nor when Hoskins got out, nor when the dog went berserk.

Littlewolf opened the door as Constable Hoskins approached. He held a rifle in his left hand and the dog's collar in his right. The dog lunged at the visitor, unleashing a string of slobber that settled on Littlewolf's hand.

"Caleb, if you let go of that dog, I'm gonna shoot him." Hoskins' hand dropped to the revolver at his hip. "I ain't jokin' here."

"Didn't know it was you, Abe. I'll put him in the house."

The dog fought him all the way, twisting and turning despite his master's curses. Finally, Littlewolf threw the animal into the house and slammed the door. Far from discouraged, the dog continued to bark and growl as Caleb Littlewolf, still holding the rifle, walked back into the yard.

"So," Littlewolf asked, "what brings you 'round? You got any good news for a change?"

"Nope, not a bit." Hoskins was the larger of the two men, but Littlewolf was younger and obviously more fit. As far as Faith could tell, neither man was afraid of the other, despite the tension being thick enough to cut.

"Well, then, what's the bad news?"

"The bad news is that things have gotten out of hand. Barns burned, folks bein' shot at… This ain't what I signed on for."

"What's this got to do with me, Abe? The way I see it, ol' Red-Moon was the victim of a huntin' accident. Just one of them things."

"And his barn? Was that an accident, too?"

"That old man don't hardly know whether he's comin' or goin'. Prob'ly left a lantern burnin' and went to bed."

When Hoskins finally responded, his tone was crisp. He sounded, to Faith, like a man with a job to do. "Thing is, Caleb, Ben Hightower found a bullet out in the yard. When I left him, the bullet was in his pocket and there was a twelve-gauge shotgun in his hands. Aunt Eva, she's got herself a shotgun, too, and I can tell you from experience that she knows how to use it."

Littlewolf laughed deep down in his chest. "Am I supposed to be worried?"

"That all depends. See, that bullet can be matched to the rifle it come out of. And one other thing. The way I heard tell, that woman who's been stayin' at Aunt Eva's, the one with the kid? She was in Stroudsburg this afternoon, talkin' to the sheriff. So if it was me had the huntin' accident, I'd make sure to ditch the gun I used before some fool jury misinterprets what happened to Red-Moon and arrives at a different conclusion."

For once, Littlewolf was impressed. He lowered his head and stared at the ground for a moment. Then he said, "Yeah, alright, I get the message. And I guess I got to thank you for deliverin' it."

"Finally, you're talkin' sense. Now, Red-Moon woke up for a little while this afternoon. He says he don't know who shot him. Fact, he don't remember anything after eatin' his breakfast. That's all to the good, but, like I said, the violence has got to stop. I hope you're listenin' close, Caleb. Any more trouble, I'm gonna take it personally."

"You tell that to Gore?"

"Yes, I did. Enough is enough."

From inside the house, Littlewolf's dog began to howl in frustration, so great was its urge to sink its teeth into Constable Hoskins' flesh.

Faith knew that Paul Crow was evidence, too; getting rid of him would be as essential as getting rid of the rifle used to shoot Red-Moon.

Those thoughts tore through Faith's mind as she listened to the fading sounds of Abe Hoskins' car. Caleb Littlewolf was already in the house, shouting at his dog. She was left alone with a growing sense of urgency—and of doom. There was no leaving now, but the task ahead of her seemed hopeless. Even if Paul was still alive, hidden in one of the outbuildings, she'd never get across the yard without being discovered by the dog. The smaller of the outbuildings, the tool shed, was on the far side of the house and the prevailing breeze would carry her scent right to the dog's sensitive nostrils. Game over.

Faith watched a rabbit hop into the yard and begin to feed on the new grass, its ears constantly revolving as the creature monitored its surroundings. Another animal hunted by almost every predator in the forest. Faith looked across the yard at her owl, but the bird didn't so much as glance at the rabbit. From inside the house, the dog began to bark wildly. A moment later, the door opened and the dog, shortly followed by Caleb Littlewolf, tore out of the house. The rabbit's head shot up and it began to run, fleeing into the woods. As before, the dog followed at a gallop, ignoring his master's command to stop.

Littlewolf remained where he was for a moment, scanning the backyard, his rifle cradled in his arms. Maybe he was tempted to let the dog go, to cut his losses. That would be a disaster for Faith. Left to his own devices, the animal would eventually discover her presence. But then Littlewolf, still cursing, trotted off in pursuit. Apparently, he didn't have far to go, most likely because the rabbit had sought the safety of its burrow, leaving the dog to howl in frustration.

"Dang you, dog," Caleb complained as he hauled the animal across the yard and back into the house. "I got you to protect me against people, not no dang rabbits. You keep this up, I'm gonna tie a rock to your neck and drop you in the lake."

Twenty-Three

LEFT TO HERSELF, Faith Covington settled down. The sun had vanished, leaving a swatch of gold on the far horizon that gradually darkened into a smoldering ember. The wind flowed through the forest, commanding every living cell to accommodate its power. The leaves and branches overhead danced to the wind's tune. The grasses and weeds in the yard were bent nearly to the ground. Faith pulled her jacket tight around her body and turned up the collar.

Another good reason to go for help, she told herself. Then she laughed softly. *Funny how the forest, which had seemed so friendly this afternoon, could become threatening only a few hours later.* It was moodier than a teenage girl—at least that's what her mother would say.

She looked up to discover that the stars had emerged, millions upon millions of them, and the great splash of the Milky Way ran from horizon to horizon, a silvery rainbow dividing the night sky.

From across the yard, the owl chose that moment to sound its haunting call. *Hoo, hoo, hooooooo.* The dog began to bark inside the house, growing more and more frenzied until the door opened and Caleb Littlewolf emerged, this time with a firm grasp of the dog's collar. He took a brief look around before deciding no one was there and dragging the dog inside.

Again, the owl called, and again the dog began to bark, but Littlewolf didn't come out this time. Faith heard him yell at the dog, heard the dog yelp, but the door stayed closed. It remained that way even when the owl's hoot rolled through the forest, over and over and over again.

Faith looked across the clearing. The owl was no more than a faint shadow, but she was sure the bird's eyes were fixed on her. The message was clear, in any event. There would be no response to the dog's alarms. Caleb had grown tired of that game.

The sun was down and the moon had yet to rise. This was as dark as the night would get, which wasn't—Faith had to admit—all that dark. A light in Littlewolf's kitchen cast a wedge of illumination across the yard, a wedge she would have to cross in order to reach the barn.

Faith didn't move, either to advance or to retreat. In her heart of hearts, she knew she couldn't leave without at least trying to find Paul. There were only the two small buildings, after all. But the fear that descended upon her was only an inch from terror. She was the rabbit, the squirrel; she was every hunted animal in the forest. One mistake, that was all it took. One mistake was the difference between being dead or alive. Any field mouse knew that. If Caleb Littlewolf got his hands on Faith Covington, he'd kill her—assuming his dog didn't kill her first.

Summoning all her courage, Faith rose to her feet. The wind pulled at her hair, slid beneath her jacket. It brought tears to her eyes. *Run*, she told herself, *and don't slow down until you reach the barn. If you show some courage and stop thinking of yourself as a child, you'll be able to search both buildings in a matter of minutes. You can always go for help if you don't find Paul.*

That last thought got her moving. Only a few minutes' work and she could retreat to the safety, not to mention the warmth, of Red-Moon's cozy kitchen. Faith drew in a long breath then ran through the wedge of light and across the clearing, feeling entirely conspicuous. Did the dog detect her presence? She would never know. The owl was hooting away, and the dog never stopped barking. Faith could see Littlewolf, now, through the window. He was seated before a small table, a bottle of whiskey at his elbow, a glass in his hand.

Good, she thought, *let him get so drunk he falls on his face. In fact, let him get the dog drunk, too.*

Faith wrapped her fingers around the handle of the barn's rolling door and pulled. The door creaked softly as it slid a few inches, and Faith, unable to control herself, let go. She looked back at the house. Caleb Littlewolf had not moved. Grimacing, Faith pulled again on the handle, this time putting her back into it, and the door opened far enough for her to slip into the building. She pulled the door closed before taking a look around.

Or not taking a look around. The windowless space was so dark that she couldn't see her hand in front of her face.

"Paul?" she whispered.

No answer. Which didn't mean anything if Paul was gagged. Or did it? Faith closed her eyes for moment as she ordered herself to think. Somehow, she had to put aside the emotions—especially the fear—that swirled through her mind and body. Caution might be a good idea; caution prevented you from doing really stupid things like walking along the edge of a roof, or riding the back bumper of a Third Avenue bus. But caution and its cousin, fear, were useless now that she was committed. Now she had to think straight.

Still unable to see anything, Faith listened to the sounds outside, the owl's call, the dog's response, but most of all the rush of the wind, which seemed to her at that moment to carry the life of the earth as it plunged into the future. She imagined the wind rolling over New Jersey and New York, the wind roiling the waters of the Atlantic Ocean as it roiled the waters of Wildwood Lake. She imagined ships on the ocean besieged by crashing waves, captains sailing into the face of the wind. There were no guarantees out there, as there'd been no guarantee that her life would be safe and secure. The world was filled with dangers. To be human, ultimately, was to face them with courage, whatever the outcome.

At last able to control her thoughts, Faith finally realized the obvious. Even if Paul was tied and gagged, he'd make some kind of noise at the sound of her voice. Kick the wall, bang his head against the floor, something.

"Paul?" This time she spoke loud enough to be heard in every corner of the barn. But, again, there was no response.

Faith drew a mental picture of her route from the barn to the little tool shed, no more than fifty feet away: Slide the barn door open just far enough to get out, close the door, which was visible from Littlewolf's kitchen window, dash across the flat ground and disappear into the shadows. It would take ten seconds, at the most, and if the tool shed was unoccupied, she'd be finished. She could retreat with honor.

As plans go, Faith's was perfectly reasonable. Yet, like any plan, it could not protect her from unforeseen hazards like the rusting shovel lying in the grass. As Faith ran, she tripped over the shovel's handle and went down hard.

Stunned for just a second, she finally crawled the last twenty feet on her hands and knees, ignoring a pair of sharp pains in her right knee and right shoulder.

Caleb Littlewolf hadn't heard her—that was the good news. His front door remained closed. The dog, however, set up a frenzied barking that was echoed by the equally relentless call of the owl. The bird was only a few feet away now, hanging on the branch of a tree right behind the tool shed. It stared directly at her, its eyes as cold and unforgiving as the wind spinning through her hair. She watched the animal's beak open and close as it called, imagined that beak tearing into the carcass of its prey, and shuddered.

Faith moved up to the shed's door, only to find it secured with a heavy padlock. She smiled. Locked doors were unknown in the community; according to Aunt Eva, the People didn't steal from each other. Yet, Littlewolf had chosen to lock this door and not the door to his barn. He was hiding something.

The implications were obvious and Faith didn't spend any time considering them. Not only could she be seen from the kitchen window, the moon had cleared the treetops and the whole yard was brightening. If Littlewolf came out of the house, she'd be spotted in a second. She scurried around the corner, placing the shed between her and the house, and began a methodical search for a way into the tool shed, perhaps a loose or missing board. She didn't stop until she came upon a large knothole in the pine siding.

Faith put her eye to the knothole. She didn't expect to see much of anything; like the barn, the tool shed had no windows. So when she found another eye staring back at her, she cried out before she could check herself. Inside the house, the dog exploded.

"Paul?"

"Faith?"

"I've come to get you out of here. We don't have any time to waste."

"You haven't come alone, have you?"

"I had to because I didn't know you were here." Faith put her mouth to the knothole and lowered her voice. Describing the events and the paths that brought her to the shed was out of the question now. "Look, there's a padlock on the door. Can you move around?"

"My hands and feet are tied. I can get to my knees, but that's about it. You need to go for help."

"Not without you. There's got to be a way in there."

"Well, you could try tearing the lock off with your teeth."

Was that a joke? Faith shook her head, sure of two things. Paul Crow had a very strange sense of comic timing. And, unlike the council, they didn't have time for a debate.

She continued to circle the building, testing the vertical pine boards, hoping to find one loose enough to pry open. She was halfway around when she finally noticed that the foundation was composed entirely of concrete blocks and the blocks were resting on the ground. There was no reason she couldn't dig beneath them. All she had to do was cross the yard and retrieve the shovel she'd tripped over. She could see it lying in the grass, no more than twenty feet from where she crouched.

Faith hesitated just long enough to visualize the task. Then she dashed across the yard, snatched up the shovel and dashed back toward the shed. She was within a few feet when Caleb Littlewolf's front door opened.

"Is anybody out there?"

Faith vanished into the shadows behind the shed an instant before the owl rose from its perch, providing a distraction and protecting her and Paul. The bird flew directly over her head and glided across the yard, passing within a few feet of Littlewolf's head, calling as it went. *Hoo, hoo, hooooooo.* Littlewolf flinched, but held onto the dog's collar. His rifle was tucked beneath his free arm, the weapon useless unless he let the dog go.

"C'mon, dog, git back inside 'fore I lose my temper. I got a job to do tonight and I don't want any more of your foolishness. You wanna chase owls, you better learn how to fly."

Faith did everything she could to keep the noise down. She placed the shovel's blade on the ground and pushed gently with her foot. But the task was hopeless and she knew it within seconds. The shovel didn't penetrate the rocky ground more than an inch and the scraping of metal on rock was painfully loud.

Now what? Give up and go for help? Suppose she did exactly that. Suppose she brought Ben and Aunt Eva back here and found the shed empty. How would she live with herself if she abandoned Paul, and if Littlewolf acted before she returned? Briefly, she considered using the shovel as a weapon. There was nothing she'd like more than to crack the shovel into Littlewolf's knees. But there was the dog to consider. And that rifle.

You're giving in again, she told herself. *You're starting to panic. You need to relax and reevaluate. Make sure you haven't missed anything. You weren't led all this way for nothing.*

As if in agreement, the owl, now perched on Caleb Littlewolf's roof, hooted twice. The dog barked as well, though probably not in assent. Faith laid the shovel down and again circled the shed, testing boards as she went, until she reached the padlocked door. The moon was up now, flooding the yard with light, and the padlock was clearly visible. But it wasn't the lock that drew her attention. No, the lock was obviously new. The hasp, on the other hand, was so rusted it might have been installed when the shed was first constructed, and the screws holding it to the frame had loosened up a bit. There was a space between the hasp and pine siding, space enough for the blade of a shovel.

Faith made her way back to the knothole. "Paul?" she whispered.

"I'm here."

"Look, is there any way you can get loose? I want to pry the lock off, but if I make a lot of noise, we'll have to get out of here in a big hurry."

"I've been trying to get loose ever since Caleb put me in here, with nothing to show for it except sore wrists. But even if I could, there's another problem. I twisted my ankle back in the woods, which is how Caleb caught me in the first place. I don't think I can run."

"Can you walk?"

"I won't know that for sure until I get these ropes off. Do you have that pocket knife I gave you?"

Faith tapped her pocket. Paul had given the folding knife to her one afternoon when they were fishing. As gifts go, it meant a lot. But as knives go, it wasn't much. The larger of its two blades was missing and the ivory bone handle was cracked in several places. Faith used it mainly to trim the line after tying off bobbers and hooks.

"Yes, I have it."

"I'm going to turn my back and put my hands up against the knothole. You open the knife and slide it through. Maybe I can cut my way free."

Faith did as she was told. Handling the knife by the blade, she pushed it through the small opening and waited for him to grasp the handle. Then she hesitated only long enough to check the house. The door was closed, but from this angle, she couldn't see the table in Littlewolf's kitchen.

Not that it mattered. The owl was crying now, its single mournful note sounding on and on as a call to action. The time for planning was over. So why, despite the cold wind, was her body drenched in sweat?

Faith stayed close to the side of the shed as she circled the building, shovel in hand, all the way to the front door. Carefully, but without hesitation, she forced the blade of the shovel between the pine boards and the hasp before applying a steady pressure at the very end of the handle. Three screws secured the hasp. At first, they slowly gave way, but then they dug in, forcing Faith to apply more pressure. The resistance was maddening.

Bathed in moonlight, she was completely exposed. If Littlewolf looked out the window, if he opened the door to check, as he had just a few minutes before, she'd be spotted in a flash. There would be no escape.

Please God, she whispered, *and all you saints and angels—and if there are any Lenape spirits out there—if anyone's listening, please, please, please, let me get this door open.*

Faith's prayer was answered, but not in the way she'd hoped. The screws never did let go. Instead, the shovel tore off a chunk of siding, the crack of the exploding wood seeming as loud as a thunderclap. Almost as an afterthought, the door swung wide and Paul stumbled out. Behind Faith, the dog began to snarl and growl, a new urgency to its tone. She could hear its nails scratching against the door of the house.

Faith put an arm around Paul's shoulder and led him toward the woods. She didn't head back the way she'd come, not to the ancient road that ran to the mine, but to the edge of the forest closest to the shed, the one that would lead them to Red-Moon's house.

Even so, they had to cross fifty feet of moonlit yard. Although Paul was moving as fast as he could, it seemed as if they were running underwater, as if the shadows at the edge of the forest were retreating instead of advancing. Still, they'd almost made it, almost lost themselves in the enveloping darkness, when a voice sounded behind them, Caleb Littlewolf's voice.

"You, stop right there, you dang kids. You stop or I'll let this dog loose."

The words flew across the yard to strike Faith's ears, sharp as bee stings. But she didn't stop, and neither did Paul. If anything, the boy took the lead, plunging into the trees an instant ahead of his rescuer. He led Faith along a path that wound between a patch of sharp-thorned briars, until they came to a grove of mature pine trees. Then he stopped abruptly in the center of the grove. The lowest branches of the pines were well above their heads and the trees grew far apart. Covered with fallen needles, the space was open. At least they would see the dog coming.

"We can't outrun the dog," Paul announced. "We have to stand our ground. But we should still have time."

"Time? What are you talking about?" Faith found Paul's calmness maddening. Somehow, he didn't seem at all worried.

"The dog'll be on us long before Caleb. That gives us time to handle the dog and still get away."

Handle the dog? Faith was thinking more about how dogs can't climb trees and that maybe she should get up in one. Then she watched Paul lift a fallen branch from the forest floor and trim off the narrow end until he was left with a solid chunk of wood, a virtual club, three feet long and several inches thick.

"That dog," he explained, "is no different from his master. He's a bully and a coward. It don't matter how fierce he looks. That's all for show. He won't fight if he doesn't think he can win."

Faith watched in disbelief. She could hear the dog now—growling, snarling, crashing through the brush, taking the straightest possible route to its quarry. The animal would break through the tangle of shrubbery at the edge of the pine grove within seconds. In the far distance, a beam of light played on the trees. Caleb Littlewolf was lagging behind with a flashlight. By the time he arrived to pull the dog off of them...

Run, run, run! The single word sounded in Faith's mind with the clarity of a church bell. If the dog overcame Paul, at least one of them would be alive to tell the tale. But she didn't move. Instead, she bent to pick up a rock and felt instantly calmed. Before she could ask herself why, the dog broke into the open, white teeth bared, running full speed ahead.

"C'mon, dog," Paul said. "Come and say hello."

The black lab didn't hesitate. He came straight for Paul Crow, leaping at his throat without slowing down. At the very last second, Paul stepped aside and brought the club down on the animal's back. The dog's cry, a mix of surprise and rage and pain, echoed in the forest, blotting out the rush of the wind. He tumbled to the side, regaining his feet, turning once again to face his adversary.

"Don't make me hit you again, fella," Paul begged.

But the wheels were turning now and the animal barely hesitated before resuming the attack, a painful error. Paul stepped forward and brought the club down on the dog's nose, the most sensitive part of its body.

This time the big lab's agonized yelp was about pain and nothing else. When Paul stepped in closer, raising the club above his head, the dog turned and disappeared as fast as it had arrived. Its path took it right past Faith, but she might have been another tree for all the interest the animal showed in her.

"C'mon, Faith, we have to get out of here before Caleb shows up."

Faith, who'd come all this way to rescue Paul, found herself being led through the woods like a lost child. What she'd just witnessed was so extraordinary that she couldn't process it. Her thoughts were whipping through her mind.

Not Paul, though. He led her along a path visible only to himself, his confidence so infectious that she almost came to believe that they'd made a successful escape.

Almost.

Twenty-Four

CALEB LITTLEWOLF WAS not Crease Marron, who seemed utterly lost in the woods. Traitor or not, Littlewolf was a Lenape. The forest was not his enemy, and if he wasn't as intimately familiar with the forest trails as Paul, he at least had a flashlight to make up for it. The moon had seemed as bright as the sun back in the clearing around Littlewolf's house. That, as Faith Covington now realized, was an illusion. In the deeply shadowed forest, the light barely reached the ground. They couldn't move, even on the little trails, without making noise.

Nor could they move very fast. Paul was in obvious pain. Though he did his best not to show it, he winced with every step. Faith put her arm around his shoulder to help him along, which only slowed their progress further. Behind them, the beam from Caleb Littlewolf's flashlight continued to sweep the woods. They could hear him now, though he didn't call out, didn't threaten or curse them. He hunted in silence, so obviously determined that Faith never even considered the possibility of surrender. Escape or die, those were her choices.

So they continued on, crossing ground totally unfamiliar to Faith, with Paul showing the way. He avoided marshes and clearings of any kind, his path twisting and turning, until their lead gradually increased, until what had been hope became actual confidence in Faith's mind, until she dared to imagine Littlewolf under arrest, Littlewolf made to pay for his crimes. Then Paul tripped over a tree branch and fell to the ground. To his credit, he didn't cry out and managed to rise. But even with Faith's help, he couldn't put his right foot on the ground.

Briefly, Faith tried to go on, half-dragging Paul along. But it was no good. Off in the distance, she heard the call of an owl. *Hoo, hoo, hooooooo.* Its cry reminded her of a truth she'd stumbled upon earlier. She had been sent to find Paul and to bring him home, not the other way around. To do that, she'd have to take control, to act on her own, every consequence flowing from her own decisions.

"Leave me here," Paul said. "Go for help."

"That's exactly what I intend to do, only maybe not the way you're thinking. You see those pine trees over there?" Faith pointed to a small grove of young pines, their branches so intertwined they might have been the extremities of a single organism.

"I see them, but I won't hide, Faith. That's not the way."

"Oh, yes, you will, Paul Crow. Because if you don't, I'm going to stay here with you. I won't leave you to fight on your own. Clubs are all well and good for dogs, but they don't work on men with guns." Faith wrapped her arm around Paul's waist. "Now, come on. We don't have to time to argue."

Paul went along, hopping more than walking. Their progress was painfully slow and the swaying beam of light behind them crept closer. Parting the branches slowed them further, and Faith was sure Littlewolf would find them before she got away. She was completely unprepared for the two deer that crashed through the trees on the other side of the grove. Speed, not silence, was their strategy for escaping danger. Their hooves sounded on the forest floor, a series of retreating thuds that undoubtedly confused Littlewolf as much as it did Faith.

"I'll come back soon," she told Paul. "I swear it."

Originally, Faith had intended to make as much noise as possible. If necessary, she'd throw rocks into the woods or break branches with her hands in order to attract Littlewolf's attention. She had to convince him that she and Paul were still on the run. But none of that was necessary. Faith had no idea where she was and the little trails she attempted to follow turned out to be dead ends that left her to fight through the trees and brush, making noise every step of the way. Littlewolf's flashlight beam followed, flashing through the leaves, the eye of the enemy.

As Faith continued to flee—for how long she did not know, all sense of time having dissolved—a growing fatigue seized her, a fatigue that threatened to become exhaustion, all the miles she'd traveled taking their inevitable toll. Over time, the urge to seek a hiding place, to hope she wasn't discovered, grew stronger and stronger. But like any other animal, like the owl that continued to call, always a bit ahead of her, Faith feared a trap. She tried to concentrate on the hope that just beyond the next grove of trees, she'd stumble upon familiar territory.

As Faith slowed, as her energies drained, Caleb Littlewolf continued to advance, the beam of light growing closer, until Faith, in desperation, plunged into a laurel thicket. The woody shrubs rose above her head, concealing her even as the tightly interwoven branches ripped at her legs. She held her arms in front of her face, leaving her forearms and the backs of her hands to pay the price, and plunged on.

Within seconds, she was totally lost. The darkness within the thicket would have been near absolute, even if she hadn't been protecting her eyes with her hands. *Well,* she thought, *at least the same conditions apply to Littlewolf.* He, too, would become lost in there. If she were first to find her way out, she'd gain time, perhaps enough time to finally lose herself in the forest.

But Littlewolf was too smart to take the bait. He recognized the laurel thicket for what it was, a nearly impenetrable tangle that even deer refused to enter. When he got to the edge of the laurel, he began to circle, calling as he went.

"Hey, Paul, you better come on out, you and that fool girl, because I'm getting real sick of chasin' you. Use your head, boy, you got no place to run."

Instinctively, as though Littlewolf's gun were aimed at her head, Faith dropped to her knees, only to discover, to her amazement, that this is where she'd belonged from the beginning. The laurel branches did not reach the ground; she could see out between the individual plants.

"Tell me somethin', Paul. Tell me why you had to stick your nose into my business. I didn't start out wantin' to see anybody get hurt. I even convinced Scranton Properties to offer the People more than the land was worth. Then you and Red-Moon had to go messin' with my plans. Now look what's happened."

Even as she began to crawl, Faith registered her amazement. Littlewolf was blaming Paul and Red-Moon, as if Red-Moon had shot himself, as if Paul had asked to be kidnapped. Was the man crazy? But this was a question that didn't have to be answered. In the short time since she and her mother boarded the Hoboken ferry, Faith had been bombarded with situations entirely new and strange. Caleb Littlewolf, in his own way, was the strangest of all.

In the distance, an owl began to call. Faith might, only hours earlier, have taken its call for an assent. But now she read something else in that single note, endlessly stretched out, and she began to crawl in the owl's direction, following the sound until she reached the edge of the laurel thicket.

Littlewolf, as dim, apparently, as he was deluded, continued to speak as he circled. "What's your name again, little girl? Whatever. I got to admit that you got spunk. Maybe you can talk to your buddy, convince Paul to come out 'fore things go too far and somebody gets hurt."

Faith nearly laughed out loud. *What a dunce*, she thought. *He doesn't know that Paul's not here or that Paul will eventually make his way home.* But even worse, for Littlewolf, anyway, was the simple fact that all his talking was giving away his position. Faith knew where he was, and was able to wait until he was on the far side of the thicket before she broke into the open, running on fear-driven feet.

Behind her, Caleb Littlewolf cursed. Ahead of her, an owl called.

A gust of wind, powerful enough to knock her off-balance, ripped through the trees. Faith was following a path, expecting it to end, as had all the many paths she'd taken, somewhere in the deep woods. Instead, a hundred yards further on, she found herself at the edge of a marshy pond. She pulled back—the marsh was open ground and she wanted to put as many trees as possible between herself and Littlewolf. But then she saw, on the far side, a gray owl perched on the branch of a shagbark hickory tree. The owl called to her, its head slowly turning to the left until it was gazing off into the distance.

Faith looked over her shoulder. The beam of Littlewolf's flashlight moved relentlessly forward, cutting across the space between them like a sword. *Calm yourself*, she demanded. *Calm yourself.* But the message was lost in the danger of the moment. She had to act, to cross the marsh, hoping the owl was a messenger and not some dumb bird.

"I don't know where you think you're goin', but the forest runs on forever in these parts," Littlewolf shouted. "Come sunrise, you'll still be out here. You'll still be out here and I'll still be comin' after ya."

Faith held fast for a few more seconds as she plotted a course through the marsh, a series of rocks projecting above the surface. She wasn't sure how far they extended or whether she could leap from one to another, given how far apart they were. But she took the first step anyway, and then the second, then the third, onto flat rocks that accepted her weight.

In her heart, she knew her good luck couldn't continue, and she was right. The fourth rock wobbled when she stepped down, plunging her, off-balance, into the muck.

Instinctively, Faith started to rise, but she stopped herself while she was still on one knee. She'd never get to the other side if her feet sank into the mud with every step. But on her hands and knees, with her weight spread out, she could move forward…slowly, of course.

In places she was nearly swimming. But she made progress, the trees at the edge of the marsh gradually drawing closer, until Faith was almost certain that she was going to reach the enveloping shadows of the forest, unseen once again.

Then the crack of a rifle blotted out the steady moan of the wind. And the whine of a bullet passed within inches of Faith's head, sounding like the buzz of an angry hornet. Faith cried out, but didn't stop crawling. With thirty feet still to go, she knew she didn't have much of a chance. She was out in the open. There was nowhere to hide.

Then the owl rose up, flapping its wings twice, before settling into a steady glide, talons extended, coming straight at Caleb Littlewolf's face. Littlewolf ducked away in time to save his sight, but lost Faith in the process. She was out of the water and into the woods before he got off another shot.

Faith was under no illusion. She was soaking wet and the cold wind felt like a million icy needles against her skin. To stay warm, she'd have to keep moving. But she had no idea where she was or where she was going. A hundred yards away, Littlewolf's flashlight was pointed down as he picked his way around the marsh. Now that he'd shot at her once, there was no doubt as to what he'd do if he caught her.

Despite each of these factors, or all of them collectively, Faith was no longer afraid. Vividly, she recalled the construction of the Empire State Building, all the photos in the *Journal-American*. Digging the foundation, pouring the concrete, assembling the girders, installing high-speed elevators, and central air conditioning—there was an order to every stage, a procedure worked out by humans for the benefit of other humans. That order didn't apply here, in the forest, in the darkness, in the wild. Something else was going on, something unimaginably large, something beyond the temporal life of tree and leaf. She was part of it, certainly, but it wasn't about her. No, not at all.

Faith started out again, traveling perhaps fifty yards before her attention was drawn to a familiar sound, rendered nearly inaudible by the relentless winds, the babble of water over rocks. An idea began to form as she picked her way around a birch tree to discover a stream. Barely a foot wide and no more than a few inches deep, the stream was probably fed by the marsh. But where the stream came from wasn't the point. The only issue was whether or not the stream emptied, as so many did, into Wildwood Lake.

With no better option in sight, Faith began to follow the narrow stream. The going wasn't easy. Tree branches grew across the water, blocking her way, and the streambed was littered with rocks, large and small. Nevertheless, she was encouraged when she came to a depression where the water had pooled. On the far side of the pool, the water flowed over a rocky shelf, its volume greatly increased.

Fifteen minutes later, Faith was still following the stream when she rounded a bend to discover an enormous rock with a small tree growing from its face, a formation she instantly recognized as the Schnozz. She was only minutes from the Indian settlement on Wildwood Lake.

Faith glanced over her shoulder. Caleb Littlewolf was still following, but he'd lost ground. That was unacceptable. Faith wanted him to follow her; she was the one setting the trap now.

She picked up a slender branch and broke it over her knee. The flashlight's beam swung in her direction and she heard Littlewolf begin to move toward her. When he came within thirty yards, she moved off, making as much noise as possible, using familiar trails that led her, step by step, to the little farm called home by Elvin Red-Moon.

Finally, Faith burst into the moonlit yard, running for Red-Moon's house now, as fast as she could, only to slip on the dew-slicked grass and fall heavily. That was not part of the plan.

Littlewolf came into view before she could rise, his rifle cradled in his arms. He stopped abruptly, his gaze falling on Faith, sharp as a razor. Surely, he must have seen the writing on the wall, known that any action he took now would be heard, yet his rage wouldn't let him accept the obvious. His dreams of wealth were over; he would, almost certainly, spend many years in a jail cell for Paul's kidnapping, if not for the attack on Red-Moon.

All he had left now was revenge.

That was the only thought running through Faith's mind as she watched Caleb Littlewolf drop the flashlight to the ground and lift the rifle to his shoulder. *I've ruined his dream; he won't stop until he gets his revenge.* Instinctively, she shut her eyes and began to pray.

"Now, you stop right there." The voice boomed from behind her.

Faith's head jerked around as though someone had released a spring holding it in place. A tall man wearing a double-breasted suit stood a few feet from Red-Moon's porch, a sheriff's star pinned to the breast pocket of his wool jacket. He held a revolver in his hand, pointed at the ground. Alongside him, a uniformed deputy stood with his legs apart, cradling a shotgun in his arms. To the deputy's right, Aunt Eva stood next to Ben Hightower, who stood next to Judson Crow. They, too, were armed.

It was, for Faith, a beautiful sight.

"Ain't gonna tell you again," Sheriff Garber said, his gun still at his side. "You don't drop that rifle, you won't walk away."

"She trespassed on my land," Caleb Littlewolf shouted, the statement so ridiculous he barely got the last word out.

Then the sheriff made good on his threat. Without repeating himself, he raised his revolver and leveled it on Littlewolf's chest, casting whatever remained of Littlewolf's anger, not to mention his courage, into some distant corner of his brain. Caleb Littlewolf threw his rifle to the ground and raised his hands.

"Don't shoot," he begged, falling to his knees in exhaustion. "Don't shoot."

Twenty-Five

FAITH COVINGTON WOULD have made her old Schuyler Academy proud, should any if its staff happen upon her just then. She knew that was unlikely, given that she was standing on a dock in Hoboken, New Jersey, waiting for the ferry that would carry her to Manhattan, but she also knew that stranger things have happened.

Faith wore a gray cotton dress and a hat, a cloche that fit nicely over the braids pulled along the side of her head. Her black shoes were highly polished; her white socks with their lace trim were wrinkle-free. Faith had looked at herself in the mirror after dressing that morning. She was going home, back to New York City, to her now-employed father, and she had to again play the role of a proper young lady at the public school she'd be attending.

Faith's mother, Margaret, had gone ahead one week before to prepare their new apartment. Faith might have gone with her, but she'd chosen to linger among the People until the last possible moment before school began. Now, she was traveling alone.

Despite all that happened, despite Faith being in no way the girl who'd set out for the Pocono Summit three months before, she had recognized the neatly dressed young lady in the mirror. And she recognized, as well, that her transformation had only begun.

After that night, that awful night, Faith's stern, gray owl with its mourner's coat of soft feathers vanished from her life. She'd neither seen, nor even heard, the owl from that day forward, though she'd listened for its calls. Faith understood. It had helped her through the worst of times and deserved to disappear again into the forest, where it was happiest. Besides, the only matters of any great importance to follow its disappearance had little to do with her.

Caleb Littlewolf was arrested; he was still in jail, awaiting trial. Jaspin Gore, Constable Hoskins, and Crease Marron were thoroughly investigated, but no evidence emerged to connect them with Paul's kidnapping or the attack on Red-Moon. Although free to go about their business, each had paid a price after the other white families on the lake uncovered their plans.

Jaspin Gore was a rich man by anyone's standards, the son of a son of an old-time coal baron. But his neighbors were also rich. And they'd been coming to Wildwood Lake for generations. Gore's plan—to buy out the surrounding land and strip-mine eastern Pennsylvania's best hunting ground in search of coal—infuriated them. In short order, at their collective request, the state legislature in Harrisburg passed a special law declaring every inch of land for miles around Wildwood Lake a natural resource to be preserved in perpetuity. No development would be allowed, not today, not tomorrow, not a hundred years from now. As an afterthought, the Albemarle Township's board of directors fired Abe Hoskins and Crease Marron.

The People were profoundly affected by these developments. Their community would survive, and it was nice to see the Lenape working together with their white neighbors. But this had little to do with Faith Covington's future. None of them, not even Aunt Eva, truly believed that she was fated to pursue the way of the People.

"I believe it's in you to do something big," Aunt Eva told her one day as they tended the souvenir stand in Mount Pocono. "I believe it's in you to stand up for yourself and, because of your strength, to stand up for others." She'd thought a moment then added, "You are strong and courageous. You can be whatever you want to be in life, even if you don't choose to live as an Indian."

Faith believed that the speech was intended for Aunt Eva's children as well, though they weren't around to hear it.

For the most part, Faith was content to immerse herself in the day-to-day rhythms of the community, spending long hours in the forest with Aunt Eva, or fishing with Paul Crow. Faith had all but fallen in love with the placid waters of Wildwood Lake—not to mention "in like" with her neighbor, despite the massive, one-year age difference between them. Except when it rained, she and Paul went out every evening around sunset, casting off in his dugout canoe. Only the roles had been switched; he got in first and *she* would push off, due to his sprained ankle.

Thinking of Paul just then, Faith had to smile. When his parents heard that he was alive and well, the joy that exploded on their faces had brought Faith to the verge of tears. That was all good, but there were practical matters to consider as well. Paul had to be found and Faith was the only one who knew where to look. Or did she? Faith was exhausted and not at all certain she could lead a search party from Caleb Littlewolf's house to the pine grove where she left Paul. That section of the forest was totally unfamiliar and Paul had led the way after his escape.

Fortunately, Faith was never put to that test. They were still discussing their strategy about what to do when Paul came limping into the clearing, a forked branch serving him as a crutch. But that wasn't the biggest surprise, not for Faith, anyway. No, the big black Labrador retriever, its tongue lolling to one side, that trotted alongside Paul nearly had Faith running for the closest tree.

"The dog found me out in the woods," Paul explained once his mother loosened her hug.

"He didn't attack you?"

"Uh-uh. His spirit apologized."

"Apologized?"

"For being a bully. For not finding out who he was until after he got free of Caleb Littlewolf."

There was no arguing with Paul Crow and Faith didn't try. Besides, the facts spoke for themselves. The dog's transformation, from the beast that leaped for Paul's throat to the friendly animal he finally became, was undeniable. Whether that transformation was accomplished by the liberation of his spirit or simply his removal from Littlewolf's influence didn't concern her. Especially because, in her mind, they amounted to the same thing.

Faith looked out over the waters of the Hudson, at the skyline of lower Manhattan. Nothing had really changed here in the short time she'd been gone. The same ragged beggars had approached the train whenever it stopped and she could see, in the distance, the tents of a squatters' camp on an unused pier. Her father, in his letters, wrote of a sense of emerging hope fueled by Franklin Roosevelt and his New Deal. Yet much of the misery remained. Every day, families were evicted from their homes, their belongings carried to the street and left at the curb. In the rain, in the snow, in the blazing heat of summer. It didn't matter. If you couldn't pay your rent, you were out.

Well, she would simply have to adjust to the contrast between Aunt Eva's world and New York City. Faith had grown closer to Aunt Eva as time passed, had come to understand her great aunt and to appreciate her world. With the garden planted, they'd gone out into the forest almost every day to gather its fruits: wild cranberries, ground cherries, and gooseberries; raspberries, blackberries, and blueberries by the quart; elderberries, Juneberries, and mulberries. The list went on and on. Meanwhile, the nuts on the trees, the walnuts and hickory nuts and acorns, were still ripening.

Aunt Eva often spoke of the forest as if it were a benevolent spirit offering up its fruits to all. Faith knew that was far from true. There was competition for every morsel of the forest's bounty, from chipmunks to bluebirds to more insects than Faith could count. If you hoped to gather anywhere near enough food to feed yourself, you had to know when each plant was likely to mature and where enough plants were clustered to make the effort worthwhile. And there were no guarantees. The raspberry patch that yielded quarts of fruit last year might have been dug up by a bear in the fall. And plants didn't have a calendar. In warm years, they matured earlier. If spring was long in coming, they matured later.

The uncertainties didn't discourage Aunt Eva, though very occasionally she and Faith emerged from the forest with little to show for their efforts. The same sometimes happened to Paul and Faith, as they fished on the lake for hours without being rewarded with so much as a nibble. Persistence was the key to success, proof positive being the jars of homemade preserves that lined the shelves in Aunt Eva's pantry and the huge salads prepared with the young leaves of nearly everything that grew.

The forest, Faith realized, was not a simple place in which to get along. But it was easier on its friends.

Aunt Eva's souvenir stand took up even more of Faith's time in her remaining weeks. Though she might have avoided the tedious hours at the roadside stand, she wanted to experience every aspect of Aunt Eva's world. By then, her father had found work, though he'd yet to start his new job, and Faith knew she'd soon be leaving for New York. Would she ever return to Pocono Summit? Perhaps to visit, but there were no guarantees in life.

Faith stepped back to allow the ferry passengers to disembark then stepped onto the ferry. She remained at the front of the vessel as it backed away from the dock and turned to face the colossal city across the water. As it did, she felt the past slip into the past, a collection of memories she would hold in her heart forever. She felt like she had found a piece of who she was, of who she was meant to be. She was ready for the future now, for whatever life would bring—or at least she felt more ready than she ever had.

Paul was still in search of his spirit guide and Faith truly believed he'd eventually find his way. But she'd found her own guide and it wasn't the spirit of an animal that lived in the forest. The voice that guided Faith not only came from deep within her, it spoke with a forcefulness she was unable to resist. And that voice told her it was time to come home.

The day was hot and windless, and thick with a gray haze that slowly parted as she drew closer to shore. In the distance, Faith heard the scream of a retreating police siren. The traffic along the elevated West Side Highway was snarled, as usual, and drivers were leaning on their horns. A line of yellow taxicabs, like honeybees awaiting entry to a hive, extended northward from the ferry slip. Occasionally, one pulled away, but fares were hard to come by. The subways and the buses charged a nickel for a ride that would take you almost anywhere in the city.

Faith gripped the rail as the ferry crossed the wake of a passing tugboat, rising up, plunging down. Oddly, she chose this moment to look back at the New Jersey shore. Parting with the People had been hard. Faith had gotten to know everyone in the community by the time she was ready to journey home. Harder still was saying farewell to Aunt Eva and Ben Hightower. For once, even Aunt Eva was without words.

And as for Paul? They'd said their goodbyes on the night before Faith left, out on the lake. The sunset was spectacular, highlighting long, tubular clouds with a palette of reds and yellows and an orange so vivid the clouds were transformed into waves of molten lava. Out on the water, a family of geese performed aerial drills. The little goslings of a few months before had barely learned to fly. They needed practice if they were to survive the southern migration. Ever dutiful, their parents, one flying in front, the other behind, guided the family back and forth across the lake, honking madly, much like the cars stuck in New York traffic.

Paul and Faith had fished for hours, until the sun was all the way down and the clouds were streaks of charcoal only a shade lighter than the night sky. Paul would never speak first. Faith knew that, but she struggled to find the right words: *I'll miss you? I'll never forget you?* Both were true, but they didn't begin to express the whirlpool of emotions she felt toward him at the moment.

Back in New York, Faith had never been without friends—friends she intended to contact as soon as she settled down. But Paul was alone; there were few other children his age in the community. He would inevitably turn to Red-Moon, who'd outfoxed everyone by recovering completely while remembering nothing. The entire day, from breakfast on, was a blank for him.

"Look at me, Paul," Faith had finally said in the canoe.

Paul's eyes rose from the hook he was baiting to meet hers. He didn't speak, only nodded once.

"I feel like I was meant to be here," she said, "and that I was also meant to leave. That sounds silly, as if the Depression and all my family's problems only happened so I'd come to the Poconos and meet the People, particularly you. But I can't stop thinking it's true. There are too many things I can't explain, not only about that night, but even before. I can't explain them and I don't want to. In a weird way, I feel like you saved my life instead of me saving yours."

"Guess you found your courage. That's a good thing." Looking, for once, like the twelve-year-old boy he was, Paul dropped his rod into the canoe and dug deep into his pocket.

"Here, I made this for you."

Paul reached out his hand and handed Faith a brown leather chord with a smooth black rock tied to it.

"It's a necklace—a talisman," Paul said. "Wearing it will bring you a thousand wishes."

And that was as close to a true goodbye as Paul and Faith got. They'd parted that night without even a hug and Paul had not turned up in the morning. Faith was neither surprised nor saddened. Paul Crow had a place in her heart from which he would never be expelled. That was enough.

FINDING FAITH

The ferry captain let loose a blast of his foghorn that rolled across the waters of the Hudson, a single note that reminded Faith of her owl. She raised a hand to smooth her collar and touch the talisman around her neck, the only part of her outfit not becoming a "proper" young lady. Then, at the very end of the pier, she saw her mother and father standing side by side.

"Ah," she said out loud, the one syllable telling the whole story.

The Lenape community had pronounced Faith a hero for rescuing Paul. Faith had protested at first, but then accepted the praise with a simple, "Thank you."

But now she realized something that should have been obvious from the very beginning. There were other heroes here. She could see two of them now, standing on the pier, their grins a mile wide. Margaret and Thomas Covington hadn't quit. Despite misfortunes that fell on them with the ferocity of a hailstorm, they stayed true to their hopes and to their family. Like Aunt Eva, they had made their own way and never lost faith.

The newspapers carried daily stories about the numbers of families split apart by the Depression. With no job, and no prospect of one, some fathers simply wandered off to join the army of homeless men crisscrossing the country, the hobos, the bums. But not Thomas Covington.

How lonely must he have been, watching his wife and child cross the Hudson, walking the streets and avenues in the company of the frightened and the hopeless? How had he shielded himself? What umbrella had he raised to ward off the demons of despair? In his letters, Thomas Covington had attributed his good fortune to pure luck. President Roosevelt's Federal Housing Administration just happened to be setting up shop when he was in need of a job. If the agency had been established a year earlier or a year later, he'd be another unemployed accountant in a worn suit, wrinkled shirt and scuffed shoes.

Faith knew otherwise. She knew that lucky breaks sometimes occurred, but that we ultimately created our own fortunes—good or bad—by choosing our own paths.

Still, correcting her father was the last thing on her mind at that moment. No, as the ferry slowed, she allowed herself, for the first time in many, many months, to be thirteen years old, a child again, her parent's little girl, the apple of their eye.

"*Mommyyyy, Daddyyyy,*" she called, waving across the water.

Finally, with her own spirit to guide her, Faith Covington had found her way home.

www.ingramcontent.com/pod-product-compliance
Lightning Source LLC
Chambersburg PA
CBHW030312080526
44584CB00012B/542